THE HISTORIC
SHOPS & RESTAURANTS
OF NEW YORK

✦

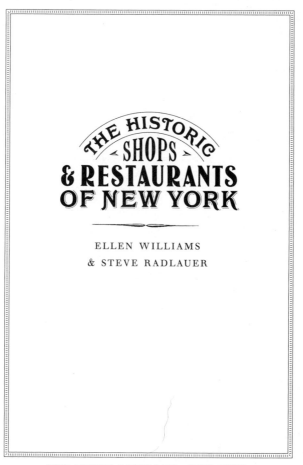

THE HISTORIC SHOPS & RESTAURANTS OF NEW YORK

ELLEN WILLIAMS
& STEVE RADLAUER

THE LITTLE BOOKROOM · NEW YORK

TO NEW YORK
YESTERDAY, TODAY, AND TOMORROW

✦

CONTENTS

INTRODUCTION

N EW YORK IS THE YOUNGEST OF THE WORLD'S GREAT CITIES. THERE IS SIMPLY LESS TAN- gible history—no classical ruins, no medieval churches, no Renaissance palaces—than in, for instance, Rome, London, or Paris. But the city's rel- ative youth does not account for the fact that so much of its 400-year past has vanished without a trace. These disappearances were deliberate, not accidental. From the beginning, New York has con- sistently, unremorsefully, plowed under the old to make way for the new.

Yet certain things do endure, even here. Every guidebook to New York will point the way to the grand, century-old monuments—City Hall, the Metropolitan Museum, the Statue of Liberty—that enshrine the civic, cultural, and philosophical ideals upon which the city was built. But there is also a surprising number of century-old commercial establishments that are harder to discover and yet, in some ways, more meaningful in the day-to-day life of the city. These are the monuments to the thrift, industry, and vision of people who, long ago, lived, worked, brought up their children, and grew old here. In the ultimate here-today-gone-tomorrow city, the oldest shops and restaurants also stand as testament to perseverance in the face of war, economic turmoil, and ever-changing tastes. These enterprises are the subject of this book.

The founding fathers and mothers of most of the places chronicled in these pages—the butchers, the bakers, the pasta and knish makers—were immigrants from many nations in pursuit of the American Dream. Their businesses, many of which started on humble pushcarts, have long outlasted them to become living landmarks that give the city a street-level sense of history that continues to nourish the present. Some of these businesses are large and some are small; some are architectural gems and some are simple storefronts. They range from world-renowned jewelers, clothiers, and fine restaurants to offbeat literary haunts, neighborhood drugstores, and delicatessens. All have successfully catered to generations of New Yorkers; many have delighted visitors as well. And because this is New York, they collectively boast an incomparable roster of celebrated former patrons, from Charles Dickens to Mae West, Thomas Edison to Al Capone, George Washington to Butch Cassidy and the Sundance Kid.

"There are living pasts and dead pasts," remarked Le Corbusier, an astute observer of the modern metropolis. New York's historic shops and restaurants, although deeply rooted in the past, are very much a living and vital presence here in the twenty-first century. They teach us about the city as it used to be and inspire our faith in its future. As we recover from the greatest assault in our history, the single most traumatic change, these enduring places provide a comforting sense of continuity as they quietly demonstrate the grace, strength, and rightness of the deeply textured, culturally diverse way of life embodied by our magnificent city.

ELLEN WILLIAMS & STEVE RADLAUER
Greenwich Village, June 2002

APOTHECARIES & PHARMACIES

✦

C. O. BIGELOW CHEMISTS

414 SIXTH AVENUE (EIGHTH-NINTH STREETS)
☎ (212) 533-2700   🚊 W. 4TH ST (A/C/E/F/V/S)
MON-FRI: 7:30AM-9PM; SAT: 8:30AM-7PM
SUN: 8:30AM-5:30PM

✦

THE OVERSIZED LEDGER BOOK DATED 1905-1906 IS FRAGILE WITH AGE. ON rare occasions, the owners of C. O. Bigelow Chemists —to remind the public that this is the nation's oldest apothecary—take it out of storage for display in one their large picture windows. More often than not, they'll open it to a page containing entries for one of their most illustrious former clients, Samuel L. Clemens, better known as Mark Twain, who, at the peak of his fame, resided around the corner at 21 Fifth Avenue. The author, the ledger indicates, was a regular customer who paid his bills promptly.

By then Bigelow was already a venerable Greenwich Village institution. As the plaque on the landmarked wall proudly states, Clarence Otis Bigelow, the proprietor in Twain's day, had acquired the shop from his former employer, who had acquired it from his former employer, who, in 1838, had established the business two doors south of the present site.

The founder chose his location wisely. "The Row," the recently built townhouses on Washington Square, just a few blocks away, was home to the social elite of New York; Jefferson Market, across Sixth Avenue, was the local center of commerce; and both the Northern Dispensary, a clinic built in 1831, where Edgar Allan Poe was a patient, and St. Vincent's Hospital, built in 1849 at Seventh Avenue and 11th Street, helped create a favorable environment for a chemist's shop. In the 1870s, the magnificent Victorian Gothic courthouse, just across the avenue, brought even more pedestrian traffic to the block.

Today, customers take pleasure in the Victorian shop fitments and ceiling moldings, and the collection of old Delftware drug jars and historic prescriptions. And they are enticed by the vivid display area, filled with an extensive and, in some cases, exclusive selection of fine European and Japanese cosmetics.

One more reason people cherish the shop: the chandeliers which, though long ago electrified, are still set up to run on gas. During the extensive East Coast blackouts of 1965 and 1977, Bigelow's was the only pharmacy from Maine to the Carolinas with sufficient light to remain open for business. It is very likely the only remaining gas-lit apothecary in the nation.

CASWELL-MASSEY

518 LEXINGTON AVENUE (48TH STREET)
☎ (212) 755-2254   🚊 51ST ST (6)
MON-FRI: 8AM-7PM; SAT: 10AM-6PM
SUN: NOON-5PM

✦

THE GREAT FRENCH TRAGEDIENNE SARAH BERNHARDT SWORE BY CASWELL-MASSEY'S Cucumber Cold Cream to remove her heavy theatrical makeup, and placed a bulk order in 1877 for 30 jars. The historic company—"America's oldest chemist"—was already accustomed to what would now be called celebrity endorsements. In 1780 George Washington presented two cases of his favorite Number 6 Cologne to the Marquis de Lafayette; First Lady Dolley Madison popularized the scent White Rose; in 1876 General George Custer cleaned his teeth before the Battle of Little Bighorn with Caswell-Massey's bone-handled Tilbury toothbrush.

The company was established in Newport, Rhode Island, in 1752, a quarter century before the American Revolution, by William Hunter, a Scottish doctor, as an apothecary shop that also sold medical supplies. During the company's first 150 years, ownership passed upon retirement from one pharmacist to another. In 1847, 17-year-old Philip Caswell, a distant relation of Abraham Lincoln, went to work for the company under the ownership of Dr. Rowland Hazard. In 1860, the first New York branch opened in the Fifth Avenue Hotel at 24th Street, 16 years before William Massey became a principal, giving the enterprise the name it has had ever since. The business flourished and by the expansive 1920s boasted as many as ten stores in New York alone, with such notables as George Gershwin and Cole Porter among the customers. The current Manhattan store, inaugurated in 1926, however, would be the sole branch in the city to survive the Great Depression.

On the shelves of that flagship store today shoppers will find flower waters, massage oils, hair products, manicure tools, bath salts, natural sea sponges, shaving brushes, mugs, creams, soaps, and aftershave gels. Imported products include Vegebom, a blend of medicinal plant extracts developed more than a century ago to treat muscle aches, minor cuts, irritations, insect bites, itching, and chapping. Caswell-Massey has been selling pure castile soap since before the Civil War. For the 250th anniversary in 2002, the company issued limited editions of a dozen of its historic fragrances, including patchouli, lavender, purple sage, red jasmine, and pomander.

KIEHL'S

109 THIRD AVENUE (13TH-14TH STREETS)
☎ (212) 677-3171   🚇 3RD AVE (L)
🚇 14TH ST/UNION SQ (4/5/6/L/N/Q/R/W)
MON-FRI: 10AM-6:30PM; SAT: 10AM-6PM

✦

THE NAME "PEAR TREE CORNER" DOESN'T MEAN MUCH TO NEW YORKERS NOWADAYS, but back in 1851 when Kiehl's first opened at Third Avenue and 13th Street, a 200-year-old survivor of Governor Peter Stuyvesant's fruit orchard was a famous local landmark. The beloved tree stood in front of the small apothecary until 1867, when it was toppled in a traffic accident between two horse-drawn wagons. By then, the shop had established a reputation for homeopathic tonics, creams, and tinctures, and for fragrances such as "Love Oil," "Money-Drawing Oil," and other botanical scents believed to confer special benefits on the wearer.

The antique scales, beakers, funnels, and colored apothecary jars that fill the deep showcase windows today recall the pharmaceutical and medicinal expertise behind the enormously popular cosmetics and skin-care formulations that have been the focus of the business for the last four decades. In a unique setting that features the original crystal-drop chandeliers hanging from a 1950s acoustic-tile ceiling, the sales staff, outfitted in white lab coats, dispense in-depth advice and generous samples of the many facial cleansers, scrubs, toners, moisturizers, masques, shaving, sun-screen, hair-care, and baby-care products.

Kiehl's continues to offer essences, including Original Musk Oil, a sample of which was discovered in the store's basement in the 1920s and, since its reintroduction in 1963, has become the most widely imitated fragrance in the world. Among the several dozen other scents are Black Narcissus, Tuberose, Cucumber, Grapefruit, and, in honor of that original landmark tree, Pear.

J. LEON LASCOFF
& SON APOTHECARY

1209 LEXINGTON AVENUE (82ND STREET)
☎ (212) 288-9500   🚇 86TH ST (4/5/6)
MON-FRI: 9AM-7PM; SAT: 9AM-4:30PM

✦

A FELLOW PHARMACIST ONCE APPROACHED J.
LEON LASCOFF WITH A PROBLEM. THE
food served at his drugstore's soda fountain was
masking the distinctive pharmacy smell that customers found so reassuring. Lascoff, who had never
offered food in his Upper East Side apothecary,
developed a winning pharmacy-scent formula of
phenol, valerian, asafetida, and iodoform, for which
his colleague was most grateful.

Since his arrival from Russia in 1892—clad in
a Prince Albert coat and silk hat among the huddled
masses yearning to breathe free—Lascoff stood out
in the crowded world of New York pharmacology.
The vine-covered brownstone that houses the drug
store he opened in 1899 is still a shrine to his
accomplishments and to his vision. A sign advising
"Silence Assures Accuracy" reminds the staff working behind the service counter and in the laboratory
of the founder's high standards; the double-story
Gothic-style windows display old photographs that

commemorate the filling of the one millionth and two millionth prescriptions—in 1936 and 1956, respectively—along with New York baseball memorabilia and the yellowing front pages of newspapers announcing the outcome of every presidential election since McKinley's. Like all pharmacies of the era, Lascoff sold leeches. Salvador Dali purchased several, not as a traditional treatment for a black eye but to use as models for a painting he was working on.

Customers who enter the shop beneath the distinctive conical copper canopy today will still find the familiar drugstore smell, along with antique mortars and pestles, pharmaceutical scales, poison flasks, and all the usual accoutrements of an upscale modern-day apothecary.

NEERGAARD PHARMACIES

120 SEVENTH AVENUE (PRESIDENT STREET),
PARK SLOPE, BROOKLYN
☎ (718) 857-1600 🚋 UNION ST (M/N/R)
454 FIFTH AVENUE (NINTH STREET),
PARK SLOPE, BROOKLYN
☎ (718) 768-0600 🚋 4TH AVE/9TH ST (F/M/N/R)
OPEN 24 HOURS/SEVEN DAYS A WEEK

✦

THE FIELDS, WOODS, LAKES, AND TRAILS OF BUCOLIC PROSPECT PARK HAD BEEN laid out for only 20 years when in 1888 Julius de Neergaard opened a pharmacy a few blocks away at the corner of Fifth Avenue and President Street. Brooklyn was still a separate city—the third largest in the nation—and Park Slope was a lovely residential neighborhood filled with gracious brownstone residences. Julius was so relentless in his devotion to the store, working every day from opening until closing, that his wife, Sara, would have to bring his lunch and dinner down to him from the family home upstairs. Only reluctantly did he allow a relief druggist to come in one afternoon and evening each week. The couple's three sons each worked in the store after school and during vacations.

[21]

Salesmen making their rounds would replenish the store's inventory of patent medicines and the chemicals and botanicals required in the preparation of medications, salves, tinctures, and tonics. Twice a month, the importer who brought leeches in from Italy would visit to clean out the water-filled jar, adding fresh ones as needed. Essential to any turn-of-the-century pharmacy, leeches were used to draw blood from black eyes and other hematomas.

In 1910, Neergaard moved the store a half-mile down Fifth Avenue, a location he was soon forced from by subway construction, ending up a few doors away at the present site. Although he was getting on in years, Julius decided to keep this store open 24 hours a day. Son William, who trained as a pharmacist and served as a medic during the First World War, took over the business upon Julius' death in 1923. He opened a branch of Neergaard's near Grand Army Plaza in 1937. The two drugstores were maintained as a family business until 1987.

IN BRIEF

BOGHEN PHARMACY, 1080 PARK AVENUE. Since 1889.

90TH STREET PHARMACY, 1260 MADISON AVENUE. Since 1890.

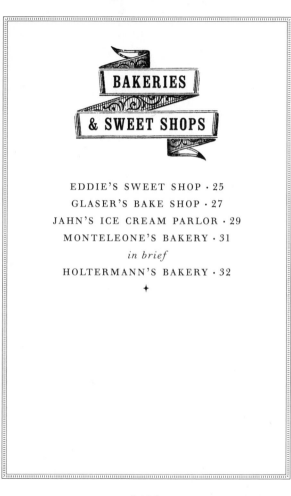

BAKERIES & SWEET SHOPS

✦

EDDIE'S SWEET SHOP

105-29 METROPOLITAN AVENUE (72ND ROAD)
FOREST HILLS, QUEENS
☎ (718) 520-8514
🚇 FOREST HILLS/71ST AVE (E/F/G/R/V)
TUE-FRI: 1PM-11:30PM; SAT-SUN: NOON-11:30PM

✦

IT DIDN'T TAKE NEW YORKERS LONG TO ACQUIRE A TASTE FOR ICE CREAM AFTER FIRST LADY Dolley Madison popularized it early in the nineteenth century, when she served it at her husband's inauguration. By 1850, Italian vendors called "hokey-pokey" men made their way through the streets of the city selling the chilled sweet stuff from small wagons that were pulled by goats. And although ice cream parlors sprang up all around town—they were one of the few types of establishments at which unaccompanied women could be served—almost none of them have survived.

Eddie's Sweet Shop in Forest Hills is an exception, preserved in near perfect turn-of-the-century condition. Nine original wood-topped revolving stools still face the mahogany counter with its cool-to-the-touch white marble top. The windows are brightened by stained-glass panels. The refrigerator is Frigidaire's first electric model, some 75 years old, and the Waring blender dates from the Second World War.

Joe and Connie Citrano, the fourth owners, have been here since the 1960s, when they took on the challenge of satisfying several generations of Eddie's customers. Appreciating the nostalgia so many people feel for the old days, the Citranos resisted any impulse to modernize the period interior. They also made a commitment to continue to serve only homemade ice cream, sherbet, syrups, and freshly whipped cream, all prepared on the premises. What they did change was the number of ice cream flavors—from just six to nearly two dozen—some of which are prepared year-round (chocolate, vanilla, coffee), some that are only available seasonally (peach, blueberry). And while most soda fountains today blur the distinction between milkshakes and malteds (which must contain genuine malt powder), and between floats and ice cream sodas (which require syrup and seltzer, never a soft drink), at Eddie's they understand the difference and continue to make each the old-fashioned way.

GLASER'S BAKE SHOP

1670 FIRST AVENUE (87TH-88TH STREETS)
☎ (212) 289-2562 🚇 86TH ST (4/5/6)
TUE-FRI: 7AM-7PM; SAT: 8AM-7PM;
SUN: 8AM-3PM

✦

THE HAMLET OF YORKVILLE HAD BEEN
ESTABLISHED IN UPPER MANHATTAN FOR
nearly half a century when first the railroad and
then a stagecoach line from New York City, then
contained within a small area at the southern tip of
the island, arrived in the 1830s. The area—centered
around what would become East 86th Street—began
to develop quickly. Although German immigrants
resided there from the start, by the turn of the century they had settled in such large numbers that the
neighborhood came to be known as Germantown.

Unlike the unskilled and working-class people
who flooded into the United States from Italy,
Ireland, and Eastern Europe, the Germans tended to
be middle-class artisans, intellectuals, and merchants. Brewers, butchers, and bakers set up along
the neighborhood's main streets, providing the beer,
bratwurst, and bread familiar from home. One of
them was John Glaser, who had run several bakeries
before buying a building on First Avenue in 1902.

[27]

Here his grandsons still prepare his recipes for Bavarian cookies, cakes, and strudels.

Viennese butter pecan, chocolate or cinnamon swirl cookies, and almond Danish are among the dozens of sweets that line the shelves of the display cases and 1918-vintage built-in oak cabinetry. Lace curtains in the windows, the original light fixtures, foxed mirrors, and the bakery's name set into the worn tile floor all create a simple yet charming period interior. Crates of raisins and nuts are stacked in the open kitchen at the rear of the shop, where the sight of bakers plying their trade recalls an earlier New York, especially on a warm day when the back door is open to the leafy back yard.

For the most part, the families of German extraction had left Yorkville by the 1960s and '70s. There are still some old-timers who shop here, though their memories of 25-cent layer cakes that now cost $45 are a mixed blessing for the owners.

JAHN'S ICE CREAM PARLOR

117-03 HILLSIDE AVENUE (MYRTLE-BESSEMER
AVENUES), RICHMOND HILL, QUEENS
☎ (718) 847-2800   🚇 121ST ST (J)
MON-THUR: 11:30AM-10PM
FRI-SAT: 11:30AM-11:30PM; SUN: 11AM-10PM

✦

THIS WELL-PRESERVED ICE CREAM PARLOR IS
PERFECTLY SUITED TO QUIET, RESIDENTIAL,
well-preserved Richmond Hill, one of the oldest
communities in Queens. John Jahn founded his
business in the Bronx in 1897 and branched out to
Queens when he felt his three children were ready
to manage shops of their own. Elsie was given a
Jahn's in Jamaica, Howard's was in Flushing, and
Frank Jahn received the Richmond Hill shop.

Although it opened in 1928, Jahn's of Richmond
Hill was meant to feel like an 1890s ice cream parlor. It still does. The interior is nearly covered in
dark wood paneling and elaborately carved embell-
ishments. An abundance of vintage sconces, each
producing a minimal amount of amber light, make
it possible to discern a grandfather clock, a remarkable marble-and-brass syrup dispenser, a Seeburg
nickelodeon, and the names and initials that generations of young patrons have carved into the paneling.

The wooden bar is topped by green marble. There is stained glass, old and new, and a gaslight street fixture that once marked the corner of Myrtle and Hillside, just outside the door. Charming oil paintings by Frank Jahn adorn each booth.

Jahn's offers a full diner menu—omelets, Belgian waffles, tuna melts, hot open turkey sandwiches, burgers and fries, fish cakes and spaghetti, fried chicken with applesauce, Hawaiian ham steaks—but it is celebrated for its way with ice cream. While it is not out of the question to have a simple scoop in one of 17 flavors, the tradition here is to go out on a limb and order one of the many eccentrically named concoctions such as the Shissel, the Bombshell, the Flaming Desire, the Boiler Maker, the Super Duper for Two, or the renowned and monumental Kitchen Sink, which serves up to eight.

The only other remaining Jahn's is in Jackson Heights at 81-04 37th Avenue. Under separate ownership, it serves the same ice cream but lacks the period charm of this location.

MONTELEONE'S BAKERY

355 COURT STREET (UNION-PRESIDENT
STREETS), CARROLL GARDENS, BROOKLYN
☏ (718) 624-9253   🚇 CARROLL ST (F/G)
MON-FRI: 7AM-9PM; SAT: 8AM-9PM
SUN: 8AM-8PM

✦

RESIDENTS OF CARROLL GARDENS DON'T NEED TO CONSULT THEIR LITURGICAL calendars to know when the religious holidays fall. They have only to pass Monteleone's on Court Street. If the bakery is selling sfingi (choux pastry filled with custard), St. Joseph's Day must be approaching; pizza grana (a deep-dish pie made with ricotta and large-grade grain) and pizza rustica (with chopped proscuitto, ham, and salami) mean that it's Easter. In the fall, there are San Martino biscuits (with fennel and anise seeds) and jelly apples. Christmas brings cassata cake (cannoli cream sandwiched between sponge cake layers and covered with fondant icing and candied fruit), rococo biscotti (with almonds and cashews), mostacciolo (chocolate-dipped ginger biscuits), and cucadate (with fresh figs and wine). In summer, Monteleone is a favorite destination for homemade Italian ices.

All the recipes are still those of brothers Frank and Harry Monteleone, who opened their bakery on nearby Columbia Street in 1902. There among cheese stores and pasta makers, they supplied the mostly Italian residents of Red Hook until the late 1950s, when the construction of the Brooklyn-Queens Expressway cut off the street from the rest of the neighborhood. Two new partners joined Harry and transplanted the business to its present location. The current owners started working for them as kids and say they feel an almost spiritual connection to the place. There may be no blood relation, and their names may not be Monteleone, but this, they will assure you, is still a family business.

IN BRIEF

HOLTERMANN'S BAKERY, 405 ARTHUR KILL ROAD, RICHMONDTOWN, STATEN ISLAND. Founded in 1878 and now run by a fourth-generation family member.

See also: CAFFÈ ROMA (P. 43), DEROBERTIS (P. 45), FERRARA (P. 48), VENIERO'S (P. 55).

BOOKSELLERS & BOOKBINDERS

✦

J. LEVINE JUDAICA

5 WEST 30TH STREET
(BROADWAY-FIFTH AVENUE)
☎ (212) 695-6888   🚇 28TH ST (N/R)
MON-WED: 9AM-6PM; THUR: 9AM-7PM
FRI: 9AM-2PM

✦

BETWEEN 1881 AND 1910 A MILLION AND A HALF JEWS FLED THE GHETTOS AND pogroms of Eastern Europe and came pouring into the port of New York. They found shelter in the squalid tenements of the Lower East Side and soon had formed the largest Jewish community in the world. Most brought with them little else but the clothes on their backs—and their devout spiritual beliefs.

In 1905, Hirsch Landy, a religious scribe, escaped with his family from the violence of Lithuania to this new American ghetto. He became a pushcart peddler specializing in essential ritual objects including tefillin (scroll containers worn while praying), talits (prayer shawls), tzitzith (special undergarments), and mezuzahs (scrolls housed in small cases for mounting on a door frame). He also made and sold Torahs—out of his home, never his pushcart—to synagogues and wealthy families.

In the 1920s, his son-in-law, Joseph Levine, took over the business and rented a storefront on Norfolk Street. At first the stock filled just a few shelves, consisting as it did of Landy's merchandise plus books—Bibles, Hebrew texts, prayer books, and a few English-language volumes. Levine clearly had a bigger idea, and rapidly expanded into manufacturing a full range of embroidered and sewn vestments for synagogues such as ark covers and Torah covers. The demand was strong, and within a short period Levine had transformed the company into a national —and even international—wholesale operation, and by far the country's leading supplier of Judaica.

Later, Levine's three sons entered the business, augmenting the store's product line with an unrivaled collection of Jewish books, items for the synagogue (menorahs, eternal lights, bar- and bat-mitzvah requisites, furniture, and chuppahs or wedding canopies), for the school (textbooks and other supplies), and for the home. By the 1960s the store, now located at Eldridge and Hester Streets, was proclaiming itself "The Department Store of Judaica." And in 1986, under the guidance of Hirsch Landy's great-grandson, the J. Levine Company opened a branch on West 30th Street. Although it was upstairs, with no storefront to showcase the goods to passersby, it was an instant success. Within a year the new place was far busier than the downtown location, which was eventually closed. The entire operation, both the factory and what is now known as "The Ultimate Judaica Store"—with its big, glitzy picture window—occupy the Midtown building.

Here are some of the things available at Levine's that were not available on Hirsch Landy's pushcart: a selection of klezmer CDs; the video *How to Trace Your Jewish Roots*; yarmulkes with embroidered football, basketball, soccer, and tennis symbols; and a mezuzah case in the form of the Empire State Building.

WEITZ, WEITZ & COLEMAN

1377 LEXINGTON AVENUE (90TH-91ST STREETS)
☎ (212) 831-2213　🚇 86TH ST (4/5/6)
MON-THUR: 9AM-7PM; FRI: 9AM-5PM
SAT: NOON-5PM

◆

THIS IS ONE OF NEW YORK'S PREMIER RARE-BOOK DEALERS—AND QUITE POSSIBLY ITS finest book bindery. The shop's roots go back to the early 1900s when Leo Weitz, from Galicia in what today is Poland, began peddling encyclopedias door-to-door to other recent immigrants. In 1909 he opened a bookstore on the Lower East Side and discovered that procuring costly, hard-to-find volumes for the rich was more fun, and more profitable, than retailing used books to the masses. His reputation grew steadily, and by the 1920s he numbered among his regular customers heirs to the Whitney fortune, automobile baron Walter Chrysler, and brewer and New York Yankees owner Jacob Ruppert, to whom he sold $100,000 worth of books in a single year. He also supplied Al Capone's library, and was compelled to appear as a witness at the gangster's trial for income-tax evasion. Weitz relocated his shop a number of times before settling in Midtown on Madison Avenue, where he remained for 30 years before moving in the mid-1960s to the present location.

Leo's son Herbert grew up surrounded by exquisite books, but did not succumb to genetic bibliophilia until about 1970, when he finally joined his father's business. On behalf of their customers, the Weitzes occasionally employed the services of local bookbinders, with mixed results. Herb corrected the situation by setting up an in-house bindery in the shop's basement, and brought in Elspeth Coleman, a designer who had been crafting book bindings since she was nine years old. With a built-in client base— and a stock of old volumes ready to be transformed into unique collectors' items—Weitz, Weitz & Coleman were soon doing a brisk trade in ultra-high-end bindings.

Today, their bindings can cost anywhere from a few hundred to several thousand dollars per volume. Aside from top-quality materials and virtuosic craftsmanship, the only common denominator is that each cover is true to its contents: a Weitz/Coleman *Rubaiyat*, for instance, is hand-tooled with Persian motifs; *Treasure Island* is adorned with a pirate's parrot; an edition of *Aesop's Fables*, illustrated by Arthur Rackham, contains a detailed rendering, in leather and gold, of one of his pictures.

The taste for these books knows no social or political boundaries. Jerry Falwell and Ted Kennedy own volumes that have been bound here, as do Yoko

Ono, Martin Scorsese, Oprah Winfrey, Mikhail Gorbachev, and Kings Olav V of Norway and Juan Carlos of Spain. And if you don't collect rare books, Weitz, Weitz & Coleman will gladly make you a custom treasure box, guest book, or, as they did for a couple celebrating their 50th anniversary, a pristine replica of a tattered wedding album.

IN BRIEF

BARNES & NOBLE, LOCATIONS THROUGHOUT THE METROPOLITAN AREA. The company started its long life in 1873 as a firm of Midwestern wholesale book jobbers who opened their first New York store at Fifth Avenue and 18th Street in 1917. Today, the nearby site of one of their superstores on Union Square occupies a literary shrine of sorts, the former home of the Century Publishing Company, where the works of Edith Wharton, Mark Twain, Rudyard Kipling, Robert Louis Stevenson, and Henry James once were produced.

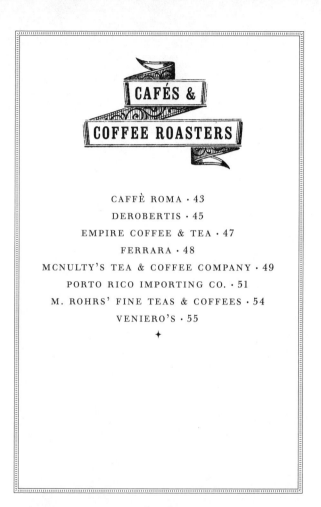

CAFÉS & COFFEE ROASTERS

✦

CAFFÈ ROMA

385 BROOME STREET (MULBERRY STREET)
☎ (212) 226-8413
🚇 SPRING ST (6); GRAND ST (S)
DAILY: 8AM-MIDNIGHT

✦

IN THE LAST DECADES OF THE NINETEENTH CENTURY, ITALIAN IMMIGRANTS ARRIVING in the port of New York quite naturally made their way to Little Italy on the Lower East Side of Manhattan. Once there, the Genoans, Tuscans, Piedmontese, and others sought out the littler Italys, the streets of their paisani. Hester Street was home to the Apulians, the Calabrasi were on Mott, the Sicilians on Elizabeth, and Mulberry Street pulsed with the heartbeat of Naples. Along with the Allevas and their latteria (p. 207), and the Mannas, who owned the restaurant Luna (p. 173), were Neapolitans like the Ronca brothers, who opened a pasticceria at the corner of Mulberry and Broome.

The Roncas ran their pastry shop until 1952, when they sold to a close friend, a fellow Neapolitan. Vincento Zeccardi, who had come to the United States in 1893 as a painter of church ceilings, was now in the Italian café business, a business that would come to sustain three generations of his family.

To change the name as little as possible, he rechristened the place Roma.

The caffè today—run by Buddy Zeccardi, Vincento's grandson—is remarkably evocative of that earlier Little Italy. There are elements dating as far back as the 1870s when the space housed a corner bar—an old saloon clock that hangs over the espresso machine, the wooden backbar behind the takeout pastry counter, the pressed-tin ceiling painted a comforting dark green like the walls. Some of the recipes—written out by hand in Italian in an old book that's kept in the kitchen—have not changed in 70 years. The current chef has been there for more than two decades, the one before that for three; the large machine that breaks up the dough predates the First World War.

The espresso and cappuccino at Caffè Roma are excellent, especially when paired with one of the classic Italian pastries—Sicilian-style cannolis, tiramisu made in the traditional Neapolitan way, sesame cookies, pignoli cookies, baba au rum, and biscotti—made with no artificial ingredients whatsoever. Special holiday cakes are made three times a year—at Easter, Thanksgiving, and Christmas.

DE ROBERTIS

176 FIRST AVENUE (TENTH-11TH STREETS)
☎ (212) 674-7137   🚇 ASTOR PL (6); 1ST AVE (L)
SUN-THUR: 9AM-11PM; FRI-SAT: 9AM-MIDNIGHT

✦

ALTHOUGH A DECADE YOUNGER THAN ITS NEIGHBOR VENIERO'S (P.55) AROUND THE corner, DeRobertis looks and feels much older. The gently worn, unreconstructed vintage interior — the original pressed-tin ceiling, the mirrors, tiled floor and walls — make the café a vivid reminder of the lively Italian community that once thrived in this part of New York. The booths at the rear have accommodated generations of espresso-sippers since 1904 when Paolo DeRobertis opened the coffee-house and bakery that he called Caffè Pugliese after his native region in the heel of Italy's boot.

Then there are the pastries — all baked on the premises — pignoli tarts, fig tarts, baba ricotta, cassatine siciliano, sfogliatella, tiramisu tarts, strawberry shortcake, boxed marzipan and chocolates, meringues, and dozens of varieties of cookies to take out. And, of course, there's the famous cannoli.

The hard-working espresso machine produces all the old standbys—delicious demitasses of hot black coffee, cappuccino, caffè macchiato—as well as steamed milk flavored with syrups such as orzata and cold drinks like iced hazelnut mochaccino. In the warm weather ices and gelati are available in flavors unknown outside the Italian parts of town.

Paolo opened his establishment the same year that Michele Lanza founded his restaurant (p. 171) a few doors to the south. In a storybook match, Paolo's son married Michele's daughter. The young couple took over the café in 1928; in about 1950 they changed the name to DeRobertis, perhaps as an inducement to their children to bond with the business. If so, it worked: their children—and their grandchildren—are now running the family's coffeehouse.

EMPIRE COFFEE & TEA

568 NINTH AVENUE (41ST-42ND STREETS)
☎ (212) 268-1220
🚇 42ND ST/PORT AUTHORITY (A/C/E)
MON-FRI: 8AM-7PM; SAT: 9AM-6:30PM
SUN: 11AM-5PM

✦

ALONGSIDE LONGTIME SURVIVORS SUCH AS MANGANARO'S ITALIAN GROCERIA (P.175) and Espositio's Meat Market (p. 122), Empire Coffee and Tea is part of today's thriving Ninth Avenue gourmet-food district. Even though the shop has moved from its original 1908 location farther up the avenue to a rather undistinguished storefront, Empire continues its tradition of roasting its own beans: American, the lightest of the roasts, produces a rich, non-bitter coffee; Viennese, somewhat darker, makes a strong, full-bodied cup; French is darker still; and Italian, the darkest roast, makes espresso. Single beans or custom blends, flavored or decaffeinated, all can be purchased whole or ground to order. The shop boasts scores of loose and boxed teas, coffee and tea accessories, and gift baskets. A few chairs at the front of the store provide a place to sip one of the daily brews. Delivery and mail order are available.

FERRARA

195 GRAND STREET (MOTT-MULBERRY STREETS)
☎ (212) 226-6150   🚇 GRAND ST (S)
DAILY: 8AM-11PM

✦

UNLIKE SO MANY ITALIANS WHO LEFT THE OLD COUNTRY SEARCHING FOR A BETTER life in America, Antonio Ferrara was a successful entrepreneur back home. From the late 1880s, the opera impresario began making voyages back and forth promoting his business. The one thing he missed while he was in New York was the lively café society he knew in Italy. In 1892, he created a place where he and other opera enthusiasts, singers, and musicians could gather after performances of Verdi or Puccini. Over the decades, his café grew to be a landmark of Little Italy.

The fourth generation of Antonio's family now runs a much-enlarged, modernized version of the original spot, with an extensive menu and a uniformed staff. In addition to cannoli, mille foglie, and biscotti, there are also strawberry shortcake, cheesecake, and an only-in-New-York drink, an Italian egg cream made with chocolate gelato and seltzer. Morning treats, sandwiches, and small pizzas are also available. Espresso can be ordered plain or laced with sambucca, Frangelico, grappa, or amaretto.

MC NULTY'S TEA & COFFEE CO.

109 CHRISTOPHER STREET
(BLEECKER-HUDSON STREETS)
☎ (212) 242-5351
🚈 CHRISTOPHER ST/SHERIDAN SQ (1/2)
MON-SAT: 10AM-9PM; SUN: 1PM-7PM

✦

KNOWN FOR YEARS AS THE SPINE OF GAY GREENWICH VILLAGE, CHRISTOPHER STREET is the oldest thoroughfare in the neighborhood, the evolution of a footpath that dated back to the waterfront Algonquin settlement of Sappokanican. In the early nineteenth century, the banks of the river were just beyond the aptly named Hudson Street, where St. Luke in the Field—today the third-oldest church building in New York—was built in 1821 at the water's edge. Here, among small farms and meandering country lanes, one business after another—saloons, poolrooms, board-inghouses, and bordellos—sprang up to meet the needs of the longshoremen who unloaded the ships docked along the Christopher Street piers, as well as the sailors in port for the day. Some of the cargo that came off those ships made it no further than the storefronts that lined the busy street.

In 1895, a McNulty's Tea & Coffee Company opened a block east of Hudson Street, offering Village residents the exotic coffee beans and tea leaves that arrived from all corners of the globe. Located on the ground floor of a six-story tenement house, the shop today betrays its considerable age in the old tin ceiling, the vintage brass scale and scoop, the bins, chests, and other antique fixtures.

The beans offered are grown in the Caribbean, Central and South America, Africa, Asia, and the Pacific. There are organic coffees, flavored coffees, decaffeinated coffees (nearly two dozen kinds), custom blends (another two dozen), and ten different brands of packaged coffees. Black teas are imported from Turkey, India, Sri Lanka, China, Russia, and Africa; green teas from China and Japan. Rare and costly Chinese white teas can sell for as much as $100 a pound. McNulty's also stocks tea bricks, house blends, flavored teas, decaffeinated varieties, 18 herbals, and packaged teas such as Jacksons of Piccadilly, Twinings, Fortnum & Mason, McGrath's of Ireland, Bewley's, Benchley, Typhoo, and Kusmi—a line of Russian blends from Paris.

PORTO RICO IMPORTING CO.

201 BLEECKER STREET
(SIXTH AVENUE-MACDOUGAL STREET)
☎ (212) 477-5421
🚇 WEST 4TH ST (A/C/E/F/S/V)
MON-FRI: 8AM-9PM; SAT: 9AM-9PM; SUN: NOON-7PM

✦

FOR A TIME, THE GENTEEL AREA OF GREENWICH VILLAGE AROUND BLEECKER and MacDougal Streets was home to such mid-nineteenth-century literary and artistic figures as James Fenimore Cooper at 145 Bleecker, Edgar Allan Poe at 85 West Third Street, Louisa May Alcott at 130 MacDougal, and Nathaniel Currier of Currier & Ives at 137 MacDougal. After the Civil War, however, as one New Yorker observed: "No street in the Metropolis has changed more than Bleecker." By 1896 a philanthropist had opened a 20-cents-a-night hostel for gentlemen of modest means at number 160, and the once-lovely residences lining the street gave way to tenement buildings that filled with waves of arriving Italian immigrants.

Italian specialty shops set up in the Bleecker Street storefronts to provide products from the old country: imported olive oils, dried mushrooms, syrups like orzata and amerina, even rolling pins for making pasta doughs. Francesco and Maria Longo opened a bakery at 201 Bleecker in 1900, selling Italian breads and preparing roasted turkeys and hams for customers who didn't have ovens in their apartments. Seven years later, another immigrant, Patsy Albanese, began marketing dark, Italian-style roasted coffee beans and stove-top espresso pots at his Porto Rico Importing Company just down the street.

By the late 1950s, the bakery had passed to the Longos' son, Angelo, and an elderly Patsy Albanese was thinking of retiring. Having spent his entire life in the family business, with its backbreaking work and punishing hours, Angelo decided to rent out the bakery and buy the coffee store. When his tenant-bakers retired in 1965, he closed the place for good and moved Porto Rico into its storefront.

This was the golden age of the Bleecker Street cafés — the Borgia, Figaro, Dante, and Reggio — where the Greenwich Village beatniks and bohemians famously gathered over espressos and cappuccinos that were brewed with Porto Rico's beans. The store continued to add new imports and new roasts; so many, in fact, that the roaster and the shipping department had to be relocated to a company-owned facility in Williamsburg, Brooklyn.

True to the family roots, the company — now in the hands of Angelo's son, Peter — operates much like a bakery, roasting only as many beans as will be needed each morning. The sacks are still warm when they arrive at the store, and may contain any one of more than a dozen special blends, four Viennese roasts, two dozen French roasts, three espressos, as well as organic coffees, two dozen decafs, and three dozen flavored coffees.

Black and green teas—from India, Sri Lanka, China, Japan—are available in great variety along with scented teas, flavored teas, spiced teas, decafs, herbals, packaged teas, and chais. In addition to all manner of brewing paraphernalia, Porto Rico sells and repairs premium espresso machines.

The company also operates two coffee bars, at 40½ St. Mark's Place in the East Village and 107 Thompson Street in SoHo.

M. ROHRS' FINE TEAS
& COFFEES

303 EAST 85TH STREET

(FIRST-SECOND AVENUES)

☎ (212) 396-4456

🚇 86TH ST (4/5/6)

SUN-WED: 7AM-9PM; THUR-SAT: 7AM-10PM

✦

IT IS NEARLY IMPOSSIBLE TO DESCRIBE THE DÉCOR OF ROHRS', A COFFEE AND TEA importer established in Yorkville in 1896. For starters, the shop—no longer in its original location—now occupies the front of an insurance agent's office. Then there's the eccentric arrangement of the space: a small area to serve yourself one of the brews of the day from insulated carafes, a minuscule seating area tucked behind makeshift room dividers, and merchandise—coffeemakers, filters, teapots, honeys, cocoa, chocolates, chocolate-covered coffee beans, biscuits—filling each and every square inch of the already cramped quarters.

The shop's original large antique coffee bins still decorate the sales counter, where several dozen coffee blends can be bought and custom-ground.

VENIERO'S

342 EAST 11TH STREET
(FIRST-SECOND AVENUES)
☎ (212) 674-7070
🚇 ASTOR PL (6); 1ST AVE (L)
SUN-THUR: 8AM-11:30PM; FRI-SAT: 8AM-12:30AM
CASH ONLY

✦

A 1944 CLIPPING FROM THE HERALD TRI-BUNE ON VENIERO'S 50TH ANNIVERSARY quotes an enthusiastic visitor who described the café as being "like something out of a fairy tale." Native-born Americans accustomed to apple pie and pound cake were dazzled by the vivid display of multicolored, unpronounceably named Italian pastries that were served with bracing black espresso.

None of this seemed unfamiliar to Antonio Veniero's first customers, fellow immigrants who had settled in this part of the Lower East Side at the end of the nineteenth century. Veniero's started as a billiard parlor that offered homemade candies and coffee laced with sambucca. The sweets were so successful that Veniero soon sent for master bakers from his native Sorrento. By the 1930s, the store's reputation far exceeded the confines of the Italian enclave. FDR's inauguration cake came from

Veniero's and newsreel footage of an art deco monument carved entirely out of sugar fashioned for the café's 40th anniversary was shown in movie theaters throughout the country. The pasticceria also won awards at the 1939 World's Fair.

A third generation of the family now operates the busy takeout counter and sit-down café. Among the colorful baked goods today are Veniero's popular bite-size miniature pastries.

CLOTHIERS & HABERDASHERS

✦

HENRI BENDEL

✦

GENERATIONS OF FASHIONABLE NEW YORKERS HAVE UNDOUBTEDLY IMAGINED HENRI Bendel as a refined Frenchman of impeccable taste, who imported the latest styles from Paris. He was, in fact, an American, born in Lafayette, Louisiana, who arrived in the city in 1896 to open a small millinery shop at the southern end of the shopping district known as the Ladies' Mile. As the carriage trade moved uptown, so did Mr. Bendel, a pioneer on 57th Street decades before Tiffany (p. 189), FAO Schwarz (p. 91), or Bergdorf Goodman (p. 61).

While stores like Macy's (p. 71) and Bloomingdale's (p. 63) grew to include furnishing, housewares, and other departments, Bendel's expanded by collecting many fine apparel boutiques under one elegant roof. Cosmetics, perfume, and jewelry were added to women's clothing and hats, and taken home by the well-heeled customers in the chic signature brown-and-white-striped shopping bag the founder designed himself. Mr. Bendel left the company to his employees after his death in 1932.

In 1991, the store relocated to the Fifth Avenue address where Cartier (p. 187) had started out at the beginning of the century. Bendel's has distinguished itself as the place to find the latest emerging young designers as well as vintage couture, the leading upscale independent beauty brands, and eclectic home décor and collectibles.

BERGDORF GOODMAN

754 FIFTH AVENUE (57TH-58TH STREETS)
☎ (212) 753-7300
🚇 5TH AVE/59TH ST (N/R/W)
MON-WED, FRI, SAT: 10AM-7PM; THUR: 10AM-8PM

✦

Ladies' Mile is the quaint name applied to the part of town where women of privilege shopped during the era of extravagance known as the Gilded Age. From Wanamaker's at Broadway and Ninth Street to Stern's at Fifth Avenue and 23rd Street, one lavish emporium after another made fortunes for merchants who could anticipate the latest styles and cater to every whim. There, among the most celebrated retailers of the era, was a tailor-furrier—working in a modest building at Broadway and 18th Street—whose name would one day be synonymous with high fashion and international chic.

Just five years after setting up his small shop in 1894, Herman Bergdorf—who partnered for a short time with a Herman Voigt at Fifth Avenue and 19th Street—took on a young apprentice tailor named Edwin Goodman. In the decade or so that they worked together they created a salon that rivaled the eminent Parisian couture houses of the time. They proudly advertised their "superior selection of woolens and materials imported for the fabrication of elegant and stylish garments in Capes, Jackets, Newmarkets and novelties for carriage and the promenade."

By the beginning of the Great War, Goodman bought out Bergdorf—who retired to France—and moved the business to larger quarters up the avenue, from which he was evicted in 1928 by the construction of Rockefeller Center. Taking its current place beside the exclusive Plaza Hotel (p. 228), Bergdorf Goodman occupied the coveted site of the former Cornelius Vanderbilt mansion at 58th Street and Fifth Avenue, with a 17-room penthouse apartment for the owner erected atop the new building. Twenty years after Goodman's death in 1953, his son Andrew sold the family business.

Since then, the store has showcased the debuts of Giorgio Armani, the launch of Donna Karan's first collection, and the American premiere of Christian Lacroix. Departments devoted to home furnishings, linens, crystal, silver, porcelain, and stationery have been added. A menswear annex faces the main store across the avenue.

BLOOMINGDALE'S

1000 THIRD AVENUE (59TH-60TH STREETS)
☎ (212) 705-2000
🚇 59TH ST/LEXINGTON AVE (4/5/6/N/R/W)
MON-FRI: 10AM-8:30PM; SAT: 10AM-7PM
SUN: 11AM-7PM

✦

AS TEDDY ROOSEVELT AND THE ROUGH RIDERS
WERE LEADING THE CHARGE DURING THE
Spanish-American War in 1898, Bloomingdale's
donated most of its men's department to the federal
government for use as a recruiting station and
granted leaves of absence with full pay to employees
who enlisted. During the First World War, the store
made an entire floor available to the Red Cross and
posted signs in the grocery department to remind
shoppers of the rationing schedule: no wheat on
Mondays and Wednesday, no meat on Tuesdays.

The store's patriotism was an extension of the
Bloomingdale family's commitment to its community—the Upper East Side of Manhattan—where
the store had conducted business for decades before
the neighborhood became fashionable. Opened in
1872 as Bloomingdale's Hoopskirt and Ladies'
Notions Shop just a few blocks from its present site,
the store had its first success importing the great

wood-framed undergarments that had been made stylish by Empress Eugenie of France. The Bloomingdale brothers, Joseph and Lyman—who lived above the store with his wife and son—at first catered to tradespeople and other blue-collar workers who liked nice things but couldn't afford to shop at most other stores. Understanding that volume sales allowed them to undercut the competition, they offered those hoopskirts for just 50 cents apiece, six-ruffle bustles at $1.25, men's shirts for 48 cents, and overcoats for $9.98.

Bloomingdale's profited enormously by its proximity to the busy Third Avenue El, which allowed people from all over the city to reach the store easily. The opening of Central Park in 1876 brought an influx of new homes and even more new customers. A decade later, the store moved three blocks up the avenue and became instrumental in making the area a major hub, lobbying for the construction of a bridge linking Queens and Manhattan at 59th Street (1909) and for a station of the Lexington Avenue subway line (1915). With innovative publicity campaigns, Bloomingdale's constantly expanded the array of merchandise it carried to include athletic equipment (tennis racquets, croquet sets, baseball bats), cameras (the Kodak Brownie of 1900 sold for $1), and books (Charles Dickens was a best-selling author); player pianos were a sensation, with Bloomingdale's the largest seller in the world. The store was the first in New York City to use the automobile to make its deliveries, and sold radios even before the first broadcast in 1920.

After the Second World War, Bloomingdale's began a long process of upgrading its image. It steadily brought in higher quality merchandise, so that by the time it celebrated its 75th anniversary in 1957, the store was well on its way to being one of the preeminent venues for fashion in New York.

BROOKS BROTHERS

346 MADISON AVENUE (44TH STREET)
☎ (212) 682-8800
🚇 42ND ST/GRAND CENTRAL STATION (4/5/6/7)
MON-SAT: 9AM-7PM (THUR TO 8PM)
SUN: NOON-6PM

✦

THE BROOKS BROTHERS ARCHIVES CONTAIN THE RECOLLECTION PROVIDED BY A FORMER employee of the two ten-hour days she had worked as a girl on the Prince Albert topcoat that was being readied for Abraham Lincoln's second inauguration in March 1865. She had painstakingly embroidered the quilted lining with an eagle holding in its beak a pennant inscribed "One Country, One Destiny." Following the assassination, a grief-stricken Mrs. Lincoln gave the coat to a favorite White House doorkeeper whose descendants passed it on to the museum at Ford's Theater, where it is now displayed.

There were several significant ties between the president and Brooks Brothers. During the vicious Draft Riots that broke out in response to Lincoln's call for troops in 1863, the store—located then on the northeast corner of Broadway and Grand Street—was a prime target of the angry mobs because it supplied uniforms for the Union army. Two years later, the building was draped in black bunting, its flag at half staff, as the president's funeral cortege slowly passed by. Lincoln had been wearing a Brooks Brothers suit when he was shot.

By then, the store was nearly 50 years old. It had opened on April 7, 1818—one month after the inauguration of James Monroe—near the teeming waterfront on the corner of Catherine and Cherry Streets. Founder Henry Sands Brooks, the son of a Connecticut doctor, would eventually be succeeded by five of his ten children—the Brooks Brothers— as the business and the city grew ever larger and moved ever northward. The company that would come to embody conservative, traditional men's clothing was actually an innovator from the beginning. In its first hundred years, Brooks was the first in America to sell ready-made suits, Shetland sweaters, polo coats, Harris tweed, madras, and, most famously, buttondown Oxford shirts, intro- duced in 1900 and still the most popular item in the store. Men in nearly every field wore Brooks. J. P. Morgan, who shopped there from childhood, was called "Jack" by the salesmen until his death. Charles Lindbergh, who carried no luggage on his historic flight to Paris, borrowed a Brooks Brothers suit from the American ambassador that he wore for days even though it didn't fit properly. F. Scott

Fitzgerald and Clark Gable were customers, as was Franklin Roosevelt, who was widely photographed at Yalta in a distinctive cape from Brooks. Some wealthy New Yorkers even outfitted their servants in uniforms tailored by the company.

The ten floors of the flagship store on Madison and 44th Street—occupied since 1915—continue to be the preeminent source for traditional American clothing for men, boys, and, since 1949, women.

Brooks Brothers is the oldest clothier in America.

LORD & TAYLOR

424 FIFTH AVENUE (38TH STREET)

☎ (212) 391-3344

🚇 34TH ST/HERALD SQ (B/D/F/N/Q/R/V/W)

MON-TUE: 10AM-7PM; WED-FRI: 10AM-8:30PM

SAT: 10AM-7PM; SUN: 11AM-6PM

✦

SAMUEL LORD, A YOUNG YORKSHIRE FOUNDRY WORKER, IMMIGRATED TO THE UNITED States and opened a modest drapery shop on Catherine Street in 1826. His wife's cousin, George Washington Taylor, soon joined him, becoming Lord's investor and partner. Together they established one of the city's most enduring businesses.

Although Taylor was the money man behind the new venture, it was Lord who was its heart and soul. In an age when all goods were transported slowly and with great difficulty, he chose his shop's location well. There, near the docks where sailing vessels unloaded their cargo, and on one of the city's busiest market streets, Lord kept the merchandise moving. With just one or two clerks to help out, the young proprietor worked tirelessly, sometimes personally making deliveries after closing time. Shortly after Taylor's return to England, Lord built a large new store on the site of a coal yard at Chrystie and

Grand Streets. It remained there until 1902 — nearly 50 years — and helped make the area the city's new shopping mecca. Employees at the Grand and Broadway branch were armed for their protection during the Draft Riots of 1863; two years later the merchandise in that store's windows was temporarily replaced with seats to allow the viewing of Abraham Lincoln's funeral cortege as it passed up Broadway. Another location, a veritable palace in cast iron at the corner of 20th Street and Broadway, placed the store in the center of the so-called Ladies' Mile, the area where wealthy women of the age shopped for their finery.

In 1914, Lord & Taylor moved into its current midtown building.

R. H. MACY & CO.

151 WEST 34TH STREET
(BROADWAY-SEVENTH AVENUE)
☎ (212) 695-4400
🚇 34TH ST/PENN STATION (1/2/3)
🚇 34TH ST/HERALD SQ (B/D/F/N/Q/R/V/W)
MON-SAT: 10AM-8:30PM; SUN: 11AM-7PM

+

T HE HOLIDAY FILM CLASSIC MIRACLE ON 34TH STREET TELLS THE STORY OF A beloved department-store Santa Claus who persuades cynical New Yorkers to believe in the magic of Christmas. One of the principal characters is a gruff but likeable "Mr. Macy," who testifies under oath that he believes his Santa to be the one and only real Santa. When the movie was released in 1947, the real R. H. Macy had been dead for 70 years.

Roland Hussey Macy, had, in fact, introduced the first in-store Santa Claus to the world in 1870. Macy, like his friend P. T. Barnum, was a colorful character and natural showman. He had joined the crew of a Nantucket whaling ship in 1837 when he was just 15 years old. Returning to dry land, he tried his hand at selling supplies in frontier California to gold rush prospectors, then to land-speculating in Wisconsin, among other things. He failed miserably at all his undertakings. Determined to keep going, he made his way to New York, and in 1858 opened a small dry-goods emporium at Sixth Avenue near 14th Street. The tally for the first day: $11.06.

From the beginning, Macy used a red star logo to promote his new enterprise, the inspiration a tattoo on this former seaman's hand. Finding success at last, he enlarged his shop's offerings and expanded into several adjoining properties. By 1877, the year he died, Macy's establishment was a true "department store" with two dozen distinct sales areas. Glassware and china were sub-contracted to two German immigrants, Isidor and Nathan Straus, who took control of the business in 1888 after a series of interim owners.

A fleet of 500 horse-drawn wagons delivered purchases throughout the city. The merchandise ranged from ladies' and men's apparel, home furnishings, foodstuffs—one employee is credited with inventing the teabag—to the latest craze, bicycles, which could be test ridden on the store's own track. By the turn of the century, Macy's had outgrown its premises and became a pioneer in the wilds of Herald Square.

The 1902 building on 34th Street was the first in the world to install escalators—the originals are still in service today. At this time Macy's made a short-lived venture into livestock sales on its new main floor. In 1924, the completion of the Seventh Avenue addition made this the "World's Largest Store," and the company celebrated with the first Macy's Parade. Three years later the signature giant helium balloons were inaugurated; for a time, they were released at the finish of the route for people to find and bring back for a reward. Canceled during World War II due to the scarcity of rubber and helium, the balloons became 650 pounds of scrap donated to the war effort. Caught up in the post-war euphoria following the Allied victory, Macy's experimented with selling automobiles, prefabricated houses, even airplanes on the ninth floor.

The 34th Street store is a registered New York City landmark.

IN BRIEF

LANE BRYANT, 222 WEST 125TH STREET. Lena Bryant was a young widow from Lithuania — an early misspelling of her first name stuck — who started making dresses in her Lower East Side apartment in 1900. She became an overnight sensation after she designed what is considered the first maternity wear in the country. Lane Bryant eventually became one of the leading manufacturers of large-size apparel.

EISENBERG & EISENBERG, 16 WEST 17TH ST. Fourth-generation descendants now run the menswear company founded by Russian immigrant Jay Eisenberg in 1898.

FISHKIN KNITWEAR, 314 GRAND ST. Cashmere sweaters are the specialty of this Lower East Side shop, which was started in 1901 by owner Buddy Fishkin's grandfather, Joseph.

A. T. HARRIS FORMALWEAR, 11 EAST 44TH ST. Abraham Harris brought bespoke men's formalwear to New York in 1892. Cutaways, tails, tuxedos, and top hats can be rented from the company that has outfitted ten U.S. presidents for state occasions.

KNOX HATS, 620 EIGHTH AVENUE. The shop today is an offshoot of Knox the Hatter on Broadway and Fulton Street, where Abraham Lincoln purchased a distinguished top hat before the career-making speech he delivered at Cooper Union in 1860.

THE TOWN SHOP, 2267 BROADWAY. Specializing in lingerie and swimwear, the shop has been in business since 1888.

DOLLS
PLAYTHINGS
& SPORTING GOODS

✦

BENNETT'S BICYCLES

517 JEWETT AVENUE (VICTORY BOULEVARD-
FOREST AVENUE), PORT RICHMOND, STATEN ISLAND
☎ (718) 447-8652　🚌 S-66
MON-FRI: 11AM-6PM (CLOSED WED)
SAT: 10AM-5PM; SUN: NOON-3PM

✦

NEW YORK CITY WENT BICYCLE-CRAZY IN THE EARLY 1890S. BICYCLE COMPANIES proliferated, and fashionably dressed young female demonstrators were hired to pedal around town promoting both the new mode of transportation and the riding schools that sought to teach the populace this exciting new skill. An 1896 exposition of two-wheelers at Madison Square Garden drew some 120,000 enthusiastic visitors.

That same year Nicholas Bennett, who had immigrated from England not long before, opened a telegraph office on Tompkins Avenue in New Brighton. Perhaps to hedge his bet, he also sold high-wheelers and other bicycles of the day. While the telegraph business went the way of the buggy whip, there is still a shop called Bennett's—now the oldest bicycle dealer on Staten Island—and it is still presided over by descendants of the founder. In 1959 the store moved from the original location to its current home about five miles away, where it carries such popular recreational-bike brands as Trek, Giant, Cannondale, and Specialized. Bennett's also stocks bike accessories, sponsors a team of amateur racers, and is well known around the borough for its excellent service department.

CAPITOL FISHING TACKLE COMPANY

218 WEST 23RD STREET
(SEVENTH-EIGHTH AVENUES)
☎ (212) 929-6132   🚇 23RD ST (1/2)
MON-SAT: 10AM-6PM; THUR TO 7:30PM

✦

WHEN THE CHELSEA WAS BUILT IN 1884, IT WAS ONE OF THE CITY'S FIRST CO-operatives as well as its tallest building. The Victorian pile was converted to a hotel in 1905, with Mark Twain, O. Henry, and Sarah Bernhardt among the early guests; later residents included Dylan Thomas, Brendan Behan, Arthur Miller, and the composer Virgil Thomson. In the 1960s it was a hotbed of the counterculture, and the location of Andy Warhol's film *Chelsea Girls*. In 1978, Sid Vicious and Nancy Spungen lived out the final, violent days of their relationship in a room here. All of which makes this a highly unlikely place to buy a fishing rod—and yet, right there in one of the hotel's storefronts, is Capitol Fishing Tackle.

Capitol started in 1897 as a cutlery store on Third Avenue around 54th Street, eventually branching into fishing gear as well. By 1966, when it moved to the Chelsea, the cutlery was gone.

Capitol now carries the largest assortment of fishing tackle in the Northeast—saltwater and fresh—for chasing everything from trout to marlin. There are nets; waders; fishing vests; boots with cleats; croakers; saltwater and freshwater flies; casting baskets; books, including *How to Fish Wrecks, Lumps, and Rock Piles*; freshwater reels; reels for giant tuna, sharks, and other big saltwater game fish; tackle boxes; fighting chairs in teak and leather; bait buckets; charts; portable scales; electronic fish finders; filleting knives; disposable cameras; tee-shirts; hats; polarized sunglasses; and insect repellent. The prices are good. Capitol buys up surplus inventory, and liquidations, and passes on the savings. What they don't have in stock they're happy to order.

THE DOLL HOSPITAL

787 LEXINGTON AVENUE (61ST-62ND STREETS)
☎ (212) 838-7527
🚇 59TH ST/LEXINGTON AVE (4/5/6/N/R/W)
MON-SAT: 10AM-6PM

✦

DORA AND ABE CHAIS ARRIVED IN NEW YORK FROM GERMANY IN THE EARLY 1880S AND set up business in a hairdressing parlor on Second Avenue and 59th Street. They would work for hours coaxing their clients' tresses into the long, complex curls that were the style of the day, a single coiffure earning them a meager 30 cents. Women often brought their young daughters, who in turn often brought their dolls—dolls with tangled, matted hair that they wanted restored to its original perfection. Despite her husband's initial reluctance, Mrs. Chais took on the extra work, at first detangling and unmatting the doll hair in the same painstaking way they treated their customers' hair. She quickly realized, however, that simply replacing the hair took just a few minutes and yet earned the same 30 cents. They arranged to have the tiny wigs that were manufactured only in Europe shipped to them. In 1900, the couple renamed their now-lucrative establishment The Doll Hospital.

The business expanded to undertake the delicate repair of all manner of injuries that befall well-used playthings — chipped porcelain fingers, cracked bisque heads, missing glass eyes, torn fabric torsos. After Teddy bears — named for the president, Theodore Roosevelt — were introduced in 1902, they began turning up for mending as well. Broken automatons — cymbal-playing animals and other toys animated by windup spring motors — were also fixed. Following World War II, the founders' grandson, Irving, taking over from his parents, began importing antique French, German, and English dolls for sale.

The shop moved several times in the immediate neighborhood before arriving at the current location on Lexington Avenue in the early 1970s. From its second-floor space, the business continues to be divided between repair and sales. Battered dolls that are used for parts lie ignominiously in piles, while valuable vintage dolls — Armaund Marseille, Schoeneau Meister, and Kestner dolls from Germany; Jumeau and Steiner dolls from France; miniature dolls; Kewpie dolls; dolls in cloth, wood, pewter, papier-maché — are displayed and available for sale. Of the cherished toys that have been left for surgery, Mr. Chais reassures their owners that The Doll Hospital hasn't lost a patient yet.

HAMMACHER SCHLEMMER

✦

IT COULD HAVE BEEN A HARDWARE STORE LIKE ANY OTHER, BUT RIGHT FROM THE start it had grander aspirations. For one thing, it wasn't merely a hardware store that William Tollner opened on the Bowery in 1848, it was a hardware and piano supplies store. For another thing, the staff was well trained, solicitous, and attired in suits and top hats. Finally, Tollner had the good sense to hire his 12-year-old nephew, William Schlemmer.

Schlemmer, who had immigrated from Germany, penniless, five years after his uncle opened for business, started out earning $2 a week hawking tools in front of the store. By the time he was 18 he had moved inside, bringing with him a friend, Alfred Hammacher, who invested the princely sum of $5,000 in the company. The store developed and maintained a reputation for stocking high-quality and hard-to-find hardware and tools, from mortise gauges and saw bummers to plumb bobs, swages, and pin punches. And it was known as an innovator. It was one of the first stores in the country to install electric lighting, and in 1878 it was listed among the initial few hundred subscribers in the first New York City telephone directory. Three years later it published its first listing of products, and today the company stands as the oldest continuous catalog publisher in America. Both Hammacher and Schlemmer had been investing in the business all along, and when they finally bought out William's uncle, in 1883, they put their own oddly euphonious names over the door.

Throughout the years the store kept growing, moving to grander locations, always staying a step ahead of the times. When the first horseless carriages arrived, and there were few service stations to keep them running, Hammacher Schlemmer created the Motorist Touring Kit, which included the materials required to repair a flat tire or blown gasket. Between then and now the company's product line has expanded well beyond hardware. The current range of offerings includes electronics, leisure and recreation, travel, home-office, automotive, kitchen, garden, patio and pool, children's toys, memorabilia, furniture, decorative accessories, and apparel.

Hammacher Schlemmer moved to its current location, with a large showroom facing East 57th Street, in 1926.

F. LOMBARDI & SONS

440-442 BAY STREET (BALTIC STREET)
STAPLETON, STATEN ISLAND
☎ (718) 447-4009   🚍 S-51, S-54, S-76
MON: 9AM-7PM; TUE, THUR: 9AM-8PM
WED, FRI: 9AM-6PM; SAT: 9AM-5PM

✦

IN 1905, THE ENTREPRENEURIAL FRANK LOMBARDI, A NATIVE OF MADDOLONE, NOT far from Naples, Italy, opened a general store in rural Granitsville, Staten Island. The store sold farm equipment, tools, guns, and bicycles to the Italian and German immigrants of the area. Among the groceries Frank carried was pasta made at his own macaroni factory. In 1914 he took on Indian motorcycles, which at the time looked like complicated bicycles and sold for $200 each.

Two-wheeled transportation soon eclipsed his other wares, and by 1927 Frank had closed the pasta works and relocated his bike shop to larger quarters on Bay Street. He moved again five years later to the company's current home just across the street. The shop was involved in cinder-track racing and the birth of the Richmond Motorcycle Club, and over the years its line included some of the greatest names in motorcycles—BMW, BSA, Matchless,

NSU, Royal Enfield — as well as Vespa scooters and Schwinn and Columbia bicycles.

By 1960 Indian was out of business and Harley-Davidsons were in such great demand that customers had to wait months to get their hands on one. The shop — now run by Frank's sons Michael and Anthony — leapt at the opportunity to drop its other brands and become the borough's exclusive Harley dealer. The Lombardis did well with the big American bikes, but the good times ended abruptly when Harley-Davidson was swallowed by a conglomerate in 1969. By the mid 1970s, when the machines were being so poorly built that they could hardly be given away, it was Lombardi's bicycle sales that kept them alive.

Harley's fortunes, and those of the shop, turned around after 1981, when a group of Harley executives bought back the cycle manufacturer. The quality of the bikes rapidly improved, and demand once again went through the roof. Today Lombardi's — now run by Frank's grandson, Michael Jr., and great-grandson, Mark Crescitelli — sells more than 260 a year. They also handle Buell bikes, deal in used cycles, maintain a service department, perform custom work, and stock a good selection of leathers, footwear, tee-shirts, and goggles.

MILLER'S HARNESS COMPANY

117 EAST 24TH STREET
(PARK-LEXINGTON AVENUES)
☎ (212) 673-1400   🚋 23RD ST (6)
MON-SAT: 10AM-6PM

◆

BY THE TIME OF THE CIVIL WAR, NEW YORK HAD THE HIGHEST CONCENTRATION OF horse-drawn vehicles of any city in the world. Department stores, vegetable stands, the ice man and the coalmonger — even the humblest business transported its goods by a horse-drawn cart. Thousands of people earned their living tending to the animals and keeping the equipment in good repair. East 24th Street between Second and Lexington Avenues was known throughout the city as "Old Stable Row." Chockablock with blacksmiths, saddlers, bridle makers, horse doctors, and dealers, it was the one of the liveliest and most colorful streets in the city.

Among the tradesmen was a harness maker, a young Jewish immigrant from the border of Russia and Poland who had arrived in Brooklyn in 1905 with nothing but a bag of tools and a new, American-sounding name. Meyer Miller's business prospered, especially on auction days when the straw-and-oat littered street was closed and the block overrun with horses and their buyers and sellers. By the mid-1920s, though, gasoline power was in, horses were out, and in the black year of 1929 Miller went bankrupt.

All was not lost, however. Even as the traditional harness business had vanished, more and more wealthy Americans were starting to ride for sport—with two dozen riding academies in Central Park alone—and to spend money on English saddles and harnesses. Despite his contempt for these frilly sporting accoutrements, Meyer raised money from friends and relatives, sailed to England, and brought back as much riding gear as he could afford. Joined by his sons, Joe and Jack, the business was reborn as a purveyor of riding requisites to what was still known as the carriage trade.

In 1939 the shop moved into a new large store-front between Park and Lexington. It was very successful, especially after World War II, when there was an explosion of interest in riding, or at least in dressing the part. One by one the other businesses on Old Stable Row closed up; only Miller's remained, expanding into wholesale and supplying tack shops around the country with riding gear and apparel. The Millers sold the business in 1975. The store moved down the street in the early 1980s, but it remains essentially as it was: a full-service equestrian supply shop, the only one in New York City.

MODELL'S SPORTING GOODS

✦

IN THE 1880S, BROTHERS MORRIS AND GEORGE MODELL FLED THE POGROMS OF CZARIST Russia for a new life in America. Like so many Jewish immigrants of that era, they immediately procured a pushcart and set up shop. Their territory of choice was lower Manhattan's Hudson River docks, their clientele sailors, their merchandise primarily clothing. By 1889 they'd salted away enough to rent a storefront at 172 West Street at Cortlandt and — with their families living behind the store — open a haberdashery. Four years later George left to start his own business buying and selling jewelry, which survives today in the form of the four Modell's pawnshops (p. 191) in Manhattan and Brooklyn. Morris stayed with clothing, helping to outfit Teddy Roosevelt's Rough Riders during the Spanish-American War in the late 1890s, then buying up surplus army clothing and selling it to the public.

In 1925, Morris's son Henry experimentally introduced golf and riding gear; he also opened some smaller, seasonal sporting-goods outlets at Brooklyn beaches and a Bronx campground. But it wasn't until the G.I.s came home from the Second World War and enthusiastically took up leisure activities that Modell's made the leap to a full-blown sporting-goods establishment.

Today, still in the hands of Morris's descendants, Modell's is a retailing empire with nearly 100 locations in New York, New Jersey, Pennsylvania, Delaware, Maryland, and Virginia. There are 20 other locations in New York City.

FAO SCHWARZ

767 FIFTH AVENUE (58TH STREET)
☎ (212) 644-9400
🚇 5TH AVE/59TH ST (N/R/W)
MON-SAT: 10AM-7PM; SUN: 11AM-6PM

✦

WHEN THE SCHWARZ BROTHERS OPENED
THEIR FIRST TOY STORE IN BALTIMORE
during the Civil War, the recently arrived family of
Germans did a brisk business selling Union flags
to patriotic Yankees. Although most Americans
made their children's playthings rather than pur-
chasing them, the Schwarzes decided to start
branches in three other cities; one brother left for
Boston, one for Philadelphia, and one, Frederick
August Otto, for New York, where he launched the
Schwarz Toy Bazaar in 1870 on Broadway between
Eighth and Ninth Streets.

European toys were unmatched by anything
produced in the United States. FAO sailed annually
to the toy fair in Leipzig, importing the finest music
boxes from Switzerland, mechanical toys from Paris,
porcelain dolls from Germany, and doll-sized baby
carriages—the first ever seen in New York—from
London. Children delighted in Schwarz's rocking
horses, miniature pewter kitchen sets, painted tin

soldiers, dollhouses, and wooden sleds. He brought the first of Margarete Steiff's stuffed animals into the country, as well as those of Adolf Gund after they were introduced in 1898. When German imports dried up during the blockades of World War I, the company forged relationships with new American toy makers such as Beatrice Alexander, the ambitious daughter of Russian immigrants on the Lower East Side, who, as Madame Alexander, began to sell her distinctive fashion dolls through Schwarz.

Despite the great success of Macy's (p. 71) first in-store Santa Claus in 1870 — the very year Schwarz opened — Frederick never employed one, maintaining that no actor was good enough for the part. By 1880, business was so strong that the store acquired larger quarters in Union Square. In 1931 it moved to Fifth Avenue and 58th Street, where it remained for another 50 years before its final stop, just across the street.

IN BRIEF

PARAGON SPORTS, 867 BROADWAY. From a single storefront in 1908, this preeminent sporting-goods destination — still owned by the founding family — now fills several buildings on the block.

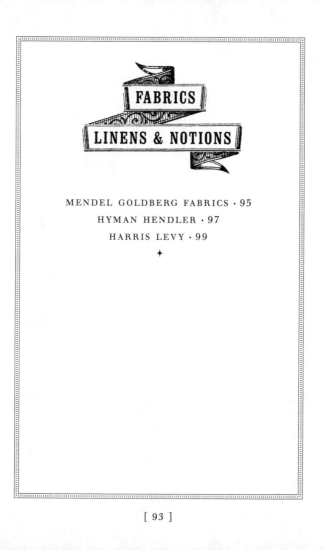

FABRICS
LINENS & NOTIONS

MENDEL GOLDBERG FABRICS

72 HESTER STREET (ALLEN-ORCHARD STREETS)
☎ (212) 925-9110   🚋 GRAND ST (S)
SUN-THUR: 9:30AM-6PM; FRI: 9:30AM-4:30 PM

✦

EACH WEEKDAY MORNING THE SWARMING
INTERSECTION OF HESTER AND LUDLOW
Streets was the site of a public "shape-up"—otherwise known as a "pig market"—where masses of
immigrant garment workers gathered to haggle
with contractors for jobs. The workers were paid by
the piece, and worked either in overcrowded sweat-
shops or, if they owned a sewing machine, in their
own overcrowded tenement apartments. Others
rented pushcarts, filled them with merchandise—
clothing, buttons, ribbons, scraps, whatnot—and
worked the streets peddling their wares.

Starting around 1890, Mendel Goldberg, a
Polish Jew with family roots in the notions end of
the garment trade, came up with a different routine.
He would visit the clothing factories of lower
Broadway and buy for a song the leftover spools of
thread for which they had no use after completing
the run of a particular garment. Goldberg then
made daily rounds of the Jewish and Italian tailors
around town—tailors with an unquenchable appetite

for inexpensive thread in every conceivable color. In time, he had saved enough to put down the sack and start his own fabric and notions store.

In the 1920s Goldberg moved the store that still bears his name to its present location on Hester Street. While it looks much as it did back then, Goldberg's grandson and great-granddaughter no longer deal in thread, buttons, zippers, or 35-cents-a-yard goods. Instead, the shop is piled with bolts from Valentino, Ungaro, Chanel, and other high-end European couture houses. And the clientele are no longer from the neighborhood but, rather, uptown ladies—and their dressmakers—seeking the finest fabric in the world for their bespoke ensembles.

HYMAN HENDLER

67 WEST 38TH STREET (FIFTH–SIXTH AVENUES)
☎ (212) 840-8393
🚇 34TH ST/HERALD SQ (B/D/F/N/Q/R/V/W)
MON-FRI: 9AM-5:30PM; SAT: 10AM-3PM
(EXCEPT JULY AND AUGUST)

✦

AT THE ULTIMATE SOURCE FOR RIBBONS, CARDBOARD BOXES ARE STACKED LITERALLY to the ceiling. They're filled with every imaginable style of ribbon—stripes, florals, ginghams, polka dots, plaids; ribbons made from satin, velvet, cotton, rayon, taffeta, needlepoint, grosgrain; jacquards woven with straight or scalloped edges—all in scores of colors and dozens of widths. Some of the merchandise is 50 or 60 years old. Much of it has been made from designs that date back hundreds of years. There are countless styles available nowhere else in the world. In fact, shops in Paris often purchase ribbons from Hendler—even ribbons that were produced in France and Switzerland.

The founder's grandchildren now run the business he began in 1900 with a pushcart on the crowded streets of the Lower East Side. The recently arrived Russian immigrant bought and sold not only ribbons but also hats, trimmings, anything he could find. He eventually moved into a loft in lower Manhattan before setting up in the current storefront—located in the center of the Midtown notions district—during the Depression. As the demand for hats has dwindled over the decades, the business mainly serves the garment industry, home furnishing designers, interior decorators, and individuals who insist on giving the most beautifully wrapped gifts in the world.

HARRIS LEVY

278 GRAND STREET
(ELDRIDGE-FORSYTH STREETS)
☎ (212) 226-3102 🚇 GRAND ST (S)
SUN-FRI: 9AM-5PM

✦

BY ALL RIGHTS, HARRIS LEVY SHOULD REALLY BE CALLED HARRIS AND ESTHER Levy, or perhaps simply Esther Levy. The couple came to the United States from the area between Poland and Russia in 1894, making the arduous voyage under terrible conditions in steerage. Harris did not weather the trip well and was sickly for the rest of his life; it therefore fell to Esther to shoulder the burden of supporting their family in the new country.

Working the Lower East Side like so many of her fellow immigrants, Esther rented a pushcart and sold fabric and linens along Orchard Street. Around the turn of the century, she rented a basement on Hester Street as a shop, cooking for her husband and six sons in the back of the store. The boys each became involved with the business; one of them worked in the store for 70 years. After their mother had retired, they moved in 1930 to a building that they bought and that the city promptly condemned. The Levys gutted the structure, spending every penny they had on rebuilding in the art deco style of the time. The contractor wanted an additional five dollars to finish the basement. It wasn't much but it was more than they had—and to this day there is only half a basement. In the early 1960s, the family purchased the adjoining building and expanded the business to include upscale bathroom accessories— the first such collection sold on the Lower East Side.

The Levys always sold premium merchandise and were importing fine linens even in the pushcart days. That tradition continues today with exclusive lines of bed, bath, and table linens, such as 1,000-thread-count Italian sheeting, hand-embroidered tablecloths, and French and Italian woven blankets. There are down comforters, pillows, and mattress pads, top-of-the-line napkins, towels, and closet accessories. Custom monogramming is a house specialty.

See also: ABC CARPET AND HOME (P. 133).

FINE ARTS & FRAMING

✦

BACHRACH PHOTOGRAPHERS

964 THIRD AVENUE, 11TH FLOOR
(57TH-58TH STREETS)   ☎ (212) 755-6233
🚇 59TH ST/LEXINGTON AVE (4/5/6/N/R/Q/W)
MON-FRI: 9AM-5PM

✦

IN 1840, SAMUEL MORSE—ARTIST, PROFESSOR, AND INVENTOR OF THE TELEGRAPH—VISITED Louis Daguerre in Paris, where he was introduced to the revolutionary new process for producing an accurate likeness with a box, a lens, and a plate coated with a chemical emulsion. Morse imported the process to New York, teaching it to others, including a gifted young man named Mathew Brady. Four years later, Brady opened the Daguerrian Miniature Gallery on Broadway and Fulton Street, just across from P. T. Barnum's American Museum. Like Barnum, Brady was a brilliant promoter. He established himself as the city's foremost photographer by doggedly pursuing, photographing, and displaying in his gallery pictures of the leading citizens of the day. It was soon considered a badge of success to be photographed by Brady of Broadway, and celebrities and commoners alike flocked to his studio. Abraham Lincoln credited his statesmanlike portrait by Brady with helping him win the presidency.

On a November day three years after that election, a large crowd gathered to attend a ceremony at a Pennsylvania battlefield. The scene was recorded by 18-year-old David Bachrach Jr., a German immigrant employed as a photographer's assistant. In the background of his picture is the speakers' platform, and on the platform sit many blurry pinpoints, one of which is Abraham Lincoln. Bachrach did not capture the president at the lectern; the short speech was over before the bulky camera could be readied, but the indistinct shot remains the only known photograph of the scene of the Gettysburg Address.

Bachrach went on to found a dynasty that would take photographic portraits of every succeeding American president—as well as generations of the world's rich and famous. Starting in 1868, the photographer ran a successful portrait studio in Baltimore. His two sons expanded the business, opening branches across the Northeast—including one in New York just after the turn of the century—codifying the Bachrach technique so that others could be trained to operate the studios. There has been a Bachrach studio in the city ever since, for those wishing to be photographed in the same regal manner as Albert Einstein, Vincent Price, E. B. White, Seiji Ozawa, and *Mad* magazine founder William M. Gaines.

JULIUS LOWY FRAME & RESTORING COMPANY

223 EAST 80TH STREET
(SECOND-THIRD AVENUES)
☎ (212) 861-8585   🚇 86TH ST (4/5/6)
MON-FRI: 9AM-5:30PM
BY APPOINTMENT ONLY

✦

OF THE OLDEST RETAIL ESTABLISHMENTS IN NEW YORK, VERY FEW ACTUALLY HAVE merchandise that is as old as they are. Julius Lowy, founded in 1907, has among its remarkable inventory items that date back to the fifteenth and sixteenth centuries. The firm's antique frame collection numbers around 4,500, with most dating from the eighteenth and nineteenth centuries.

Lowy buys and sells these historic frames, restores damaged pieces, and crafts authentic reproductions for framing works of lesser value or of dimensions that will not fit into one of the originals. A new digital-imaging system that the firm pioneered allows the image of valuable artworks to be tried in any number of scanned frames without undue wear or risk of tear to the painting itself.

In addition to its unmatched framing services, Lowy offers expert curatorial services, appraisals, and state-of-the-art conservation of paintings, works on paper, and other treasures. It is the largest and oldest fine-art services firm in the country and counts among its clients leading museums, galleries, auction houses, and corporate and private collectors.

NEW YORK CENTRAL
ART SUPPLY

62 THIRD AVENUE (TENTH-11TH STREETS)
☎ (212) 473-7705 🚇 ASTOR PL (6)
MON-SAT: 8:30AM-6:15PM; SUN: 11AM-5PM

✦

THE MEMBERS OF THE NEW YORK SCHOOL—
THE ABSTRACT EXPRESSIONISTS WHO MADE
the city the center of the international art scene
after World War II—lived, painted, hung out, and
showed their work in the low-rent eastern edges of
Greenwich Village. Jackson Pollock lived on East
Eighth, Willem De Kooning on a block of East
Tenth Street where there were five galleries. Their
bar was the Cedar Tavern on University Place and
Eighth Street. Most of the big names of the time,
and many more of the small names and no names,
found everything they needed at New York Central
Art Supply, which in the 1950s had already been
in business for half a century.

In 1905, Benjamin Steinberg, an immigrant
from Russia, began selling artists' materials and
assorted secondhand goods in this area near Cooper
Union and New York University. He and his descendants have catered to successive generations of art
students and masters by providing premium paints,

canvas, fine-art papers, an astonishing collection of brushes, and much more. During the 1950s, the family purchased the building from Peter Stuyvesant's estate, some 300 years after he had bought the land from the Dutch West India Company.

Steinberg's grandson, Steven, who remembers making bicycle deliveries to Franz Kline and De Kooning as a child, now runs New York Central. Recent customers have included Jim Dine, Frank Stella, James Rosenquist, Francesco Clemente, Jeff Koons, and Red Grooms.

There is a framing annex up the street at 102 Third Avenue.

THE OLD PRINT SHOP

150 LEXINGTON AVENUE (29TH-30TH STREETS)
☎ (212) 683-3950   🚇 28TH ST (6)
TUE-FRI: 9AM-5PM; SAT: 9AM-4PM

✦

THE PRINTS HE DEALT IN WERE ALREADY OLD IN 1898, WHEN EDWARD GOTTSCHALK founded The Old Print Shop inside Wanamaker's department store on Fourth Avenue between Ninth and Tenth Streets. Gottschalk specialized in Americana, particularly the work of the New York City firm of Currier & Ives. He soon moved into a storefront across the street, a location that was superb for his purpose. Fourth Avenue from Astor Place to Union Square was the center of the second-hand book business, and lovers of old books were often lovers of old prints as well.

Gottschalk bought prints from many sources, including "country runners" who traveled to rural flea markets, junk shops, and homes in search of sal-able treasures. One of the best runners was Harry Newman, a young man who had fallen in love with prints after discovering a cache of Currier & Ives in his grandmother's attic. Gottschalk died a few years after acquiring the building on Lexington Avenue where the shop is still located. His widow hired

Harry to run the business, which he bought in installments from 1928 to 1933.

Newman had a great eye for undervalued artists and genres. He snapped up nineteenth-century prints for anywhere from 25 cents to a few dollars apiece. In the 1930s, thanks in part to his efforts, prices skyrocketed. Just after World War II he specialized in overlooked American painters; and in the 1950s, after his son Kenneth entered the business, the shop did well with primitive art. Around 1980 Kenneth's sons joined him, Robert K. specializing in early-twentieth-century artists and printmakers, Harry Shaw II in antique maps and atlases.

Today, the stock is constantly changing, but the collection on any given day will surely include prints of old New York, botanicals, equestrian scenes, birds (including Audubon originals), beautiful old maps, portraits of American presidents, and seascapes featuring yachts, steamers, or paddleboats. The shop also provides correct period framing and offers an extensive collection of art books.

IN BRIEF

JOSEPH FISCHL, 1397 THIRD AVENUE. Now located in an Upper East Side high-rise, Fischl has dealt in artists' supplies and frames since 1892.

FISHMONGERS & BUTCHERS

✦

FAICCO ITALIAN SPECIALTIES

260 BLEECKER STREET

(LEROY-MORTON STREETS)

☎ (212) 243-1974

🚇 WEST 4TH ST (A/C/E/F/V/S)

TUE-SAT: 8:30AM-6PM; SUN: 9AM-2PM

(EXCEPT JULY AND AUGUST)

✦

ONE OF THE LAST REMAINING PUSHCART MARKETS IN NEW YORK WAS ON BLEECKER Street between Sixth and Seventh Avenues. As late as the 1970s, a solitary few fruit and vegetable peddlers stubbornly held on to a vanishing way of life. Early in the twentieth century, this part of the Village's own Little Italy was alive with curbside stands that overflowed with zucchini, fennel, olives, and other produce unfamiliar to non-Italians; the first broccoli imported to the United States is said to have been sold from a Bleecker Street pushcart. It was into this colorful setting that Faicco's Pork Store moved in 1950 after half a century doing business a few blocks away, on Thompson Street facing the church of Saint Anthony of Padua.

At the turn of the last century, when ice was the sole means of chilling food, butchers like Eduardo Faicco stocked only what could be kept fresh. Once the choicest parts of the animal were sold, customers simply bought whatever was left. The only sausages were the dried links that needed no refrigeration; the shop had no choice but to close during the hottest parts of the summer.

Today, pork roasts, chops, cutlets, and ribs are available all the time from the spotlessly clean, fully stocked, modern refrigerated showcases. Prosciutto, salami, and other cured meats have been joined by fresh sausage — hot, sweet, filled with cheese, fennel, parsley, broccoli rabe — that are made throughout the day. Because the store also sells beef and chicken and offers pastas, sauces, breads, olives, as well as a variety of prepared foods such as lasagna, eggplant parmagiana, manicotti, and meatballs, the fourth generation Faicco now in charge has changed the name of the family store to reflect its expanded merchandise.

Additional location: 6511 11th Avenue, Bensonhurst, Brooklyn.

LEONARD'S SEAFOOD
& PRIME MEATS

1385 THIRD AVENUE (78TH-79TH STREETS)
☎ (212) 744-2600　🚇 68TH ST (6)
MON-FRI: 8AM-7PM; SAT: 8AM-6PM
SUN: 11AM-6PM

✦

A MEMBER OF THE LEONARD FAMILY HAS TRAVELED TO THE FULTON FISH MARKET before dawn nearly every morning since 1910. That year, Peter Leonard, who had emigrated from Liverpool with his Irish parents when he was a baby, opened his own place selling prime meats and seafood. He had learned the fish trade as a child, starting as a pint-sized footman who opened the carriage doors of the wealthy customers at a Midtown fish market. Today, Peter Leonard's grandchildren, who moved the business to its current site in the mid-1990s, believe they have been able to survive the supermarket age because of a solid reputation based on quality and personal service.

Meats, for example, are still aged on the premises; chicken is custom cut by expert butchers and never frozen. And, in addition to all the usual meats and poultry, Leonard's also stocks fresh game (caribou, venison, wild boar, rabbit, hare) and game birds (duck, pheasant, quail, guinea hen, squab, grouse, partridge). Exotic meats (kangaroo loin, ostrich, rattlesnake, buffalo, alligator) and pheasant eggs, duck eggs, and quail eggs are all available but must be ordered in advance.

O. OTTOMANELLI & SONS

(SEVENTH AVENUE SOUTH-JONES STREET)
☎ (212) 675-4217
🚇 CHRISTOPHER ST/SHERIDAN SQ (1/2)
MON-FRI: 8AM-6:30 PM; SAT: 7:30AM-6PM

✦

MANY EUROPEAN IMMIGRANTS NEVER LOOKED BACK. OTHERS TRAVELED BACK and forth between new and old worlds. In 1900, Gennaro Ottomanelli left Bari, Italy, to seek his fortune selling cured meats from a Greenwich Village pushcart. This provided enough income to allow him occasionally to sail back home; sometimes he could even finance the travel of a few family members. Three years after Onofrio, his second son, was born in Manhattan, the boy was brought to his mother's family's farm in Bari. There he learned the butchering trade from his grandmother. In the 1930s, he returned to New York, where he and his brother, Joseph, ran the butcher shop that had supplanted Gennaro's pushcart. Not long afterward Joe decided to relocate uptown (see Ottomanelli Brothers, p. 119), while Onofrio, who loved the Village, took a storefront on Bleecker Street east of Seventh Avenue South.

There were many other butchers on that block. Onofrio needed a way to stand out if he was to succeed, and he found one: fresh game. He also supplied Italian specialties unavailable in the other shops, including lamb heads, livers, hearts, and lungs. He made his own fresh sausages, which he hung from the ceiling to age. Every day at dawn he visited the wholesale meat market, where his rapport with suppliers earned him first pick of the offerings.

His shop, O. Ottomanelli & Sons, has moved twice — in the mid-1950s one door east, 30 years later a few doors west to the present location. Apart from Faicco's (p.113), the other butchers on the block left the neighborhood or closed, while Ottomanelli's reputation continued to grow. Onofrio's four sons now run the shop, whose showcases are always stocked with poultry, homemade sausage, and beautiful cuts of prime meats dry-aged on the premises. And they remain one of the city's top game purveyors, in season carrying pheasant, quail, partridge, goose, Long Island duckling, mallard, guinea hens, poussin, rabbit, venison, buffalo, elk, alligator, suckling pig, wild boar, and kangaroo medallions.

OTTOMANELLI BROTHERS

1549 YORK AVENUE (82ND STREET)
☎ (212) 772-7900   🚇 86TH ST (4/5/6)
MON-SAT: 6:30AM-6PM; SUN: 6:30AM-6PM

✦

BECAUSE PUSHCARTS AT THE TURN OF THE LAST CENTURY HAD NO REFRIGERATION, Gennaro Ottomanelli carried only cured meat products—like prosciutto and dry sausages—that did not need to be kept cold. When Gennaro's oldest son Joseph arrived from Bari, Italy, where had been trained as a butcher on the family farm, he opened a meat store in Greenwich Village, near where his father made his rounds. When he was joined by his younger brother Onofrio, they named the shop Ottomanelli Brothers. It was a big step up from a pushcart, but it came with its own problems. The family now laughs about how Joe argued with his landlord every winter about paying for unwanted heat that only jeopardized the perishables and forced him to buy extra ice; Joe far preferred keeping the store cold and working in three layers of clothes.

Joe eventually opted to move to the Upper East Side, where there was no competition from other Italian butchers, while Onofrio remained in his own Bleecker Street shop (p. 117). The new store started out on Second Avenue and eventually moved to the present location. After a few minor name changes, Joe's sons, Joseph Jr. and Nick, changed the name back to Ottomanelli Brothers after they took over.

Ottomanelli's today is both a classic sawdust-on-the-floor butcher shop and a modern Italian gourmet shop. Its offerings include prime aged steaks and chops, lamb, and poultry; prepared foods such as lamb stew, veal chili, macaroni and cheese, grilled peppers, chicken done several ways; and breads and pastry. The Ottomanellis also produce their own line of fresh pasta — some in festive multicolored stripes — and homemade sauces.

ROSEDALE FISH MARKET

1129 LEXINGTON AVENUE (78TH-79TH STREETS)
☎ (212) 861-4323   🚇 77TH ST (6)
MON-FRI: 8AM-7PM; SAT: 8AM-6PM

✦

THE WINDOW DISPLAY AT ROSEDALE FISH MARKET—A KALEIDOSCOPIC PATCHWORK OF green-toned manilla clams, pink salmon steaks, scarlet lobsters, silver sardines, black-tipped peach-colored stone crab claws, and bright yellow lemons —is a mere hint of the variety that waits inside the shop, the oldest fishmonger in the city.

Rosedale opened on Lexington Avenue in 1906. Thirty-five years later, when it moved across the street to its current location, it had become a culinary cornerstone of the well-heeled Upper East Side. Starting out with only $250, Billy Rosedale— the current owner's grandfather — made a name for himself as a purveyor of fresh, prime seafood that he delivered all over town on a bicycle. His specialty was oysters, which are still available (Bluepoint, Kumamoto, Belon, Cape Cod, Malpeque by the dozen) along with clams, lobster, crab, scallops, shrimp, cockles, and mussels. There are dozens of whole fish, prepared items, smoked fish, caviar, seafood salads, chowders, and bisques.

Delivery is available throughout the city and fish can be shipped overnight or packed in ice to travel.

IN BRIEF

ESPOSITO'S MEAT MARKET, 500 NINTH AVE. Giovanni Esposito opened his first butcher shop in Little Italy in 1892, relocating several times before arriving, in 1932, at this location, then the site of one of the city's most colorful pushcart markets.

LOBEL'S, 1096 MADISON AVENUE. The great-grandfather of the current owners was an Austrian cattle rancher in the 1840s. The Lobel family opened their New York butcher shop, now an Upper East Side institution, in 1917.

SHATZIE'S PRIME MEATS, 1200 MADISON AVENUE. Since 1903.

FLOWER SHOPS

✦

CRESS FLORISTS

248-02 NORTHERN BOULEVARD

LITTLE NECK, QUEENS

☎ (718) 423-6255 🚌 Q-12, Q-20, Q-21

MON-SAT: 9AM-7:30PM; SUN: 9AM-5PM

✦

MOST PEOPLE THINK EITHER OF FOOD OR THE RAG TRADE—CLOTHES, BUTTONS, notions, scraps—when they picture the contents of a typical pushcart in 1900. When Thomas Cresomales arrived from Sparta, Greece, he went into flowers, trundling a pushcart in the neighborhood of Broadway and 59th Street. By 1903 he had the wherewithal to open a florist's shop on Columbus Circle, where it remained until 1955, when the city commandeered the real estate to break ground for the New York Coliseum. The dispossessed store relocated to Woodside, Queens—well positioned to profit from the sprawling cemeteries nearby—under the name Cress & Sons. In the early 1990s it moved east to its current, nearly suburban location.

The family has done well with flowers for three generations. In recent years a branch opened in the Citicorp building in Long Island City; Cress cousins operate stores in Smithtown and Port Jefferson on Long Island.

GRAMERCY PARK
FLOWER SHOP

260 THIRD AVENUE (21ST STREET)
☎ (212) 475-4989   🚇 23RD ST (6)
MON-FRI: 8:30AM-7PM; SAT: 9AM-6PM
SUN: 11AM-5PM

✦

THE PRIVILEGED TURN-OF-THE-CENTURY RESIDENTS OF GRAMERCY PARK HAD ONLY to look outside their windows to view some of the loveliest landscaping in all of New York. The flowering horse chestnut, cherry, and tulip trees, the laburnums, lilacs, dogwoods, and magnolias were fully mature then, having been planted in the late 1830s. It was into this horticulturally discerning community that the little Gramercy Park Flower Shop opened in 1904.

Peter and Spiro Sakas, brothers from Sparta, Greece, founded the shop—a bright spot in the shadow of the Third Avenue El—near the northeast corner of the park. Flower retailing was a natural for many Greek immigrants who wanted to be their own bosses in a business requiring little startup capital. Over the first decades, the Sakas brothers built up a loyal following in the neighborhood. Benjamin Sonnenberg, the public relations impresario, would order rare white anemones whenever Greta Garbo came to one of the lavish dinner parties he was famous for hosting at his brownstone mansion on the south side of the park.

When a red-brick high-rise replaced the shop's longtime home in 1956 — shortly after Peter's sons took over the business — the new generation opted to remain on the same corner site. In 1985 Tommy Sakas, Peter's grandson, assumed ownership, quickly doubling both the size of the shop and the amount of business it was doing.

In addition to a full range of fresh flowers, including exotic air-freighted imports the founders never dreamed of selling, Gramercy now carries plant stands, pottery, whimsical small fountains, candles, and other items of home décor as well as beautiful arrangements. During the holiday season, it is one of the best places in the city to find unusual ornaments.

IRENE HAYES WADLEY
& SMYTHE LEMOULT

1 ROCKEFELLER PLAZA
(49TH STREET OFF FIFTH AVENUE)
☎ (212) 247-0051
🚇 47TH ST/ROCKEFELLER CENTER (B/D/F/V)
MON-FRI: 8AM-6PM; SAT: 8AM-NOON

✦

WALT WHITMAN, WHO ONCE THRILLED TO HAVE CAUGHT SIGHT OF ABRAHAM Lincoln on Broadway, described the grieving city the day after the president's assassination: "black, black, black." When the funeral train bearing Lincoln's body stopped in New York, the ships in the harbor and most buildings were draped in black muslin; businesses were shuttered; City Hall, where the body lay in state, was hung with a sign that simply proclaimed: "The Nation Mourns." Nearly a million New Yorkers solemnly watched the four-hour-long procession that escorted the coffin to the station for the remainder of the trip to Illinois. Among the many tributes placed on the train with the president's body was an empty chair fashioned entirely of flowers. The firm of Adolph Lemoult & Sons had been honored with the commission.

Over the course of the next century, Lemoult merged with several other florists — Irene Hayes was a former Ziegfeld girl with many celebrity clients — to create a long, ungainly name that rivals those of Park Avenue law firms. Many locations around town — a shop at the piers did a brisk business in bon voyage flowers for sailing swells — were finally reduced to one, at Rockefeller Center since 1980. Here, they create arrangements for members of the entertainment, financial, legal, and communications communities. For reliable out-of-town deliveries they maintain personal relationships with florists in every market in the nation.

IN BRIEF

JAMES WEIR FLORAL COMPANY, 160 MONTAGUE STREET, BROOKLYN HEIGHTS. Founded in 1853.

HOME FITTINGS
FURNISHINGS & HARDWARE

✦

ABC CARPET & HOME

888 BROADWAY (19TH STREET)
☎ (212) 473-3000
🚇 14TH ST-UNION SQ (4/5/6/L/N/Q/R/W)
MON-FRI: 10AM-8PM; SAT: 10AM-7PM
SUN: 11AM-6:30PM

✦

AS THE NINETEENTH CENTURY DREW TO A CLOSE, THE SO-CALLED LADIES' MILE WAS in full flower. The celebrated shopping district, extending from Ninth Street and Broadway up to 23rd Street between Madison Square and Sixth Avenue, had been growing ever since R. H. Macy opened his dry goods store in 1858 on Sixth Avenue and 14th Street (p. 71). Over the years more and more retailers erected increasingly magnificent edifices in this 14-block stretch. Among the most notable were the mansard-roofed Arnold Constable store (built in 1869) on Broadway and 19th Street, and the W. and J. Sloane store (from 1882) just across Broadway.

While New York's major retailers were hiring prestigious architects, constructing temples of commerce, and vying for the patronage of a wealthy clientele, young immigrant upstarts struggled for a toehold in their new country by peddling merchandise on the Lower East Side. In 1897, one newcomer from Austria, Sam Weinrib, found a niche selling used carpeting and linoleum from a pushcart. His son later expanded that niche in a rented storefront. His grandson moved the store to grander quarters in the old Constable building. And in the 1980s, after his granddaughter and her husband joined the firm, the family bought and renovated the six-story Sloane building across the street — a fitting move, as Sloane's was once the best store in the city for rugs and upholstery. Although few New Yorkers know the name of the Austrian immigrant who sold carpet scraps from a pushcart, everyone knows the name of his descendants' business: ABC Carpet & Home.

ABC is the country's largest importer and retailer of wool carpeting, and the first place to which many New Yorkers turn when they're looking to embellish their floors. It is also the place they go for antique sideboards, silk duvet covers, Swedish beds, cashmere blankets, handblown Venetian chandeliers, chenille throws, and French copper cookware. As high-quality establishments continue to reanimate the monumental spaces erected by the original denizens of the Ladies' Mile, the Flatiron District — as it is now called — is again one of Manhattan's premier shopping and dining hubs. ABC has been a prime catalyst in this renaissance.

ARONSON'S FLOOR COVERING

135 WEST 17TH STREET
(SIXTH-SEVENTH AVENUES)
☎ (212) 243-4993   🚇 18TH ST (1/2)
MON-FRI: 9AM-6PM; SAT: 10AM-5PM

✦

WHEN THE SIRENS THAT ANNOUNCED AIR RAID DRILLS PIERCED THE NIGHT DURing World War II, Americans throughout the country knew to turn off unnecessary lights and pull down their blackout curtains. For New Yorkers, these previously unheard-of window treatments could be purchased at Aronson's, a Greenwich Village fixture that had been in business since the end of the Civil War.

In 1867, two years after arriving from Germany, Samuel Aronson opened a glazier's shop in a Bleecker Street basement. Soon he was supplying his customers with other things they requested, including hardware, lanterns, daguerreotype frames, and oilcloth carpeting—an early form of linoleum. The business grew, eventually occupying several storefronts on the pushcart-filled street. Construction of the Seventh Avenue subway in 1909 forced the store to move down the street, where the Aronsons decided to narrow the focus to floor coverings and window shades.

After a change of ownership in the 1930s, the opening of a 14th Street branch, and another ownership change in the 1960s, Aronson's moved in 1975 to its current location. In addition to a small museum's worth of old Rube Goldbergesque carpet beaters, sweepers, and all manner of pre-electric pump-action and windup cleaning contraptions on display, the store contains every manner of resilient floor covering, including wood, cork, rubber, a selection of carpeting, and linoleum.

CITY KNICKERBOCKER

781 EIGHTH AVENUE (47TH-48TH STREETS)
☎ (212) 586-3939 🚇 50TH ST (1/2/C/E)
MON-FRI: 8:30AM-5PM

✦

IN 1823, A HOUSE ON CHERRY STREET WAS THE FIRST RESIDENCE IN AMERICA TO BE equipped with gas lighting. The small city was still huddled at the foot of Manhattan Island, and the transition from candles and oil lamps was a relatively simple matter. By the time Mr. Edison invented his lightbulb in 1879, however, the city had grown enormously; and even though Fulton Street was wired for electricity within three years, the fabled gaslight era of New York persisted for some time. The burgeoning town contained countless gas fixtures, in thousands of homes, that required converting or replacing. As late as 1906, Adolph Liroff, a recent immigrant from Russia, found that he could earn a good living electrifying old gas chandeliers for his Brooklyn neighbors. Before long, heavily stocked with lamps he had bought or traded for his services, he was packing up his fixtures and tools in burlap bags and lugging them to his newly rented Manhattan workplace on 42nd Street in the heart of the glittering new theater district.

Liroff, an opera fan, was thrilled when the Metropolitan Opera House, located nearby at Broadway and 39th Street, rented some of his lights as props. Soon he was regularly working with the company's set builders to fabricate custom period-piece fixtures. By 1913, theatrical work constituted the bulk of his business.

Adolph begat Seymour, who in the 1950s moved the shop to its current address, supplying rentals to *The Milton Berle Show, The Ed Sullivan Show, Your Show of Shows,* and other hits from the golden age of television. Seymour begat Kenneth, who fashioned a chandelier for the Broadway revival of *The Diary of Anne Frank* that crashed to the floor every night—only to be reassembled for the next performance; he also expanded into propping for films. Most recently, Kenneth begat Scott, who entered the business in the 1980s—the fourth generation of Liroffs in lighting.

In addition to its show-business work, City Knickerbocker does a considerable trade with interior decorators, makes repairs, and welcomes walk-in shoppers. Its vast stock includes scores of modern, reproduction, and vintage lighting fixtures.

GARBER HARDWARE

49 EIGHTH AVENUE (JANE-HORATIO STREETS)
☎ (212) 242-9475
🚇 14TH ST (A/C/E); 8TH AVE (L)
MON-FRI: 8AM-5PM; SAT: 8AM-3PM

✦

THE CROOKED STREETS OF GREENWICH VILLAGE HAVE INTRIGUED AND VEXED visitors ever since the rest of the city was laid out in an orderly grid in the early nineteenth century. Odd geometries are created wherever these idiosyncratic little roads cross the broad, regular avenues. One such asymmetrical corner—where West Fourth Street tumbles into Eighth Avenue—has also been an intensely colored one since 1884, when Garber's set up shop with the bright orange façade that was traditional for hardware stores of the period.

Like so many Russian Jews, Joseph Garber and his family made the voyage to New York in steerage, but once here chose to settle not on the Lower East Side but in the quieter precincts of the Village. At first, the store sold paints—powdered pigments that had to be specially mixed by hand. As construction in the neighborhood boomed in the 1890s, Joseph and his son, Nathan, added plumbing supplies and building materials. A 1913 photo of four of

Nathan's children taken out front shows that the store was already advertising "housewares"—which would become the backbone of the hardware business in the new century. Only a decade later, Nathan died following a fall from a store ladder, leaving the business to his eldest son, Ralph, who ran the place until his youngest brother, Henry, graduated from college. When Hank Garber recently died, he had put in more than 80 years in the family business.

Members of the fourth and fifth generation now work in this warren of storefronts—the family took over the two adjoining properties years ago—which are stacked floor-to-ceiling with decades of accumulated merchandise. Walk around for ten minutes and you're bound to find something—adhesive-glue remover, corncob holders, vinyl tablecloths—that you didn't even know you needed.

Joseph's great-great-grandson, Nathaniel, continues to unearth Garber treasures. Recent finds include cylinders of buckshot, old screw containers made from recycled tins of World War I-era foot powder, and roll upon roll of vintage contact paper—not vintage-style, but the real thing.

GRAND BRASS LAMP PARTS

221 GRAND STREET (ELIZABETH STREET)
☎ (212) 226-2567   🚇 GRAND ST (S)
TUE-SAT: 9AM-5PM (THUR TO 7PM)

✦

WOODROW WILSON HELPED CELEBRATE THE COMPLETION OF THE TALLEST building in the world by ceremoniously throwing a switch in the White House that turned on the 80,000 lightbulbs of the majestic new Woolworth Building on Broadway and Park Place. The year was 1913, and the glowing skyscraper heralded the imminent demise of the gaslight era in New York. For most New Yorkers, this was a good sign, a sign of progress. But for those who were in the business of producing or repairing gas fixtures, it was a worrisome time indeed.

Grand Brass Lamp Parts — which had previously been in the business of supplying gas lamps and mantles — headed off extinction by embracing the age of electricity. The shop now carried, repaired, and installed electrical lights. It also expertly converted customers' obsolescent gas lamps.

The business is still in its original location, a semi-ornate Lower East Side tenement at a busy intersection not far from the Bowery lighting district and, for that matter, from the Woolworth Building. The rest of the block is slowly being engulfed by Chinatown, but Grand Brass seems so caught up in its own nitty-gritty world of electrical supplies that it doesn't seem to notice.

Visitors entering the store are greeted by a vast collection of electrical pipes leaning against the wall, followed by the "No Refunds" sign. The floor is an archeological palimpsest of old ceramic tile showing through old vinyl tile. Shelves are packed to the ceiling with arcane electrical fittings and torn-open cardboard boxes. Brass tubing leans against the shelves; lamp shades sprout from the ceiling; finials are everywhere.

The full product line — listed on the big red sign on the storefront — includes bobeches, candle cups and covers, canopies, hickeys, weights, washers and wire, spiders, spinnings, switches, and swivels.

P. E. GUERIN

23 JANE STREET
(GREENWICH-EIGHTH AVENUES)
☎ (212) 243-5270   🚇 14TH ST (1/2/3/A/C/E)
BY APPOINTMENT ONLY

✦

IF YOU SEE SOMETHING YOU JUST CAN'T LIVE WITHOUT IN THE 1914 P. E. GUERIN catalog, don't despair. They will gladly make it for you. Everything offered since the company's founding in 1857 can still be produced — not reproduced, but made by hand from the same molds, using the same techniques, in the same foundry. Guerin, which was already more than half a century old when it put out that first catalog, also crafts many remarkable items that have been added since.

Pierre Emanuel Guerin, a native of Brittany, arrived in pre-Civil War New York and set about learning the metalworking trade. After running his own small shop in four different downtown locations, he fixed on a row of three low brick buildings on a small Greenwich Village street in 1892, with room for a showroom, an office, a carriage house for the delivery horse and wagon, as well as the foundry. Guerin's reputation as a pioneer of artistic metalwork earned him such celebrated clients as the legendary architectural firm of the Gilded Age, McKim, Mead & White. For just as Stanford White relied on Louis Comfort Tiffany for stained glass, John La Farge for murals, and Augustus Saint-Gaudens for sculpture, he turned to Pierre Guerin for the finest hardware that could be made for the finest houses in New York.

Following Guerin's death in 1911, the business passed to his son E. P.—Emanuel Pierre—and then to a nephew, whose son, Andrew Ward, is the fourth-generation owner today. Custom hardware for the bath (faucets, showerheads, towel bars, paper-holders, soapholders) and the rest of the home (door knockers, door levers, doorknobs, door pulls, key plates, keyhole covers, thumb turns, push plates, hinges, locks, latches, finials, switch plates, hooks, hangers, carpet rods, drapery tiebacks, lanterns, cabinet knobs, cupboard latches), as well as sconces, small tables, and various objets d'art in a multitude of styles are still poured, filed, chased, polished, and plated, all by hand. Stock material is produced by a company foundry in Valencia, Spain.

HARRY'S FOR THE HOME

241 BAY RIDGE AVENUE (THIRD AVENUE-
RIDGE BOULEVARD), BAY RIDGE, BROOKLYN
☎ (718) 745-0730   🚇 BAY RIDGE AVE (R)
MON-SAT: 10AM-6PM; SUN: NOON-6PM

✦

IMMIGRANTS TO AMERICA OFTEN WAITED UNTIL THEY HAD A JOB AND A PLACE TO LIVE before bringing over their children from the old country. Nine-year-old Fanny Reid was an exception. Because she already spoke some English, her parents brought her with them when they left Latvia in 1882 to join relatives in Jersey City. By 1907 Fanny — whose father was a cabinet-maker — had started a furniture factory and a nickelodeon in her uncle's building. The furniture company prospered; the nickelodeon didn't.

In 1909 she crossed the Hudson River and opened a store in the heart of the Lower East Side, on Orchard Street, to sell her tables and chairs. Around 1920 she moved the store to Bay Ridge, Brooklyn, and continued to expand the business. When she died, in 1933, she left her daughter, Florence, and son-in-law, Harry Pancer, some good commercial real estate and a successful furniture company.

Harry started purchasing consignments of damaged furniture, which the store repaired and sold at wholesale prices. Soon the company was dealing with every major southern furniture maker, and by 1960 had become known as "the Loehmann's of furniture." Harry's son and then grandson entered the family enterprise, which restyled itself as a "full-line furniture department store with a focus on value." Plans are afoot to expand to Long Island to serve the suburban children, grandchildren, and even great-grandchildren of its original customers in Brooklyn and Manhattan.

WILLIAM H. JACKSON CO.

210 EAST 58TH STREET
(SECOND-THIRD AVENUES)
☎ (212) 753-9400
🚇 LEXINGTON AVE/59TH ST (4/5/6/N/R/W)
MON-FRI: 9:30AM-5PM

✦

THERE IS AN ORNATE LOUIS XV MANTEL ON DISPLAY IN THE WILLIAM H. JACKSON showroom. Five feet tall and more than seven feet wide, of marble and gilded bronze, it has been in the company's possession since the 1930s or thereabouts. Since then the shop has moved several times, and the bulky, heavy, somewhat fragile piece has moved with it. The mantel would make a perfect addition to the right—very large—room. Worth $200,000, it probably could be acquired for less considering how pleased the Jackson people would be to finally see it go.

The business was already at least 100 years old when it acquired this extraordinary French objet. All that is known about the man who founded the firm on Pearl Street in 1827 is that he made iron grates and other fireplace necessities. As the city moved uptown, so did Jackson. At some point the company opened a foundry in Brooklyn and expanded into monumental work such as cast-iron building façades and large lamps for public spaces, such as the ones still standing nearby at the Second Avenue entrance to the Queensboro Bridge. The company went bankrupt during the Depression doing work for the New York subway system; it was rescued by an investor and since then has stuck to its knitting.

Today, while there is still a small factory in Queens, William Jackson is primarily a retail fireplace specialist stocking mantels, grates and backs, iron linings, fenders, bellows, screens, and tools. The George Washington andirons they stock have been in more-or-less continuous production since the late 1700s, and are particularly endearing. The selection of mantels is astonishing, with shallow English pine-and-gesso pieces from the late eighteenth and early nineteenth centuries; rare and lovely sand-blasted cast-iron pieces from the mid-nineteenth century; French mantles of every shape, size, and period; limestone mantels painted to resemble marble; pieces molded from a variegated stone amalgam called Cretan; and many others.

PUTNAM ROLLING LADDER COMPANY

32 HOWARD STREET

(BROADWAY-LAFAYETTE STREET)

☎ (212) 226-5147

🚆 CANAL ST (6/J/M/N/Q/R/W/Z)

MON-FRI: 8:30AM-4:30PM

✦

EVER SINCE MANHATTAN REAL ESTATE
BECAME SCARCE, THE COMMON SOLUTION
has been to build up. Inside cramped city shops and
homes, where every square foot is especially precious,
the answer has been to stack—to the ceiling if need
be. To access the inaccessible, to reach the unreach-
able, several generations of New Yorkers have
turned to the Putnam Rolling Ladder Company.
Invoking the slogan "For All Kinds of Shelving
That Is More Than Man High," Samuel Putnam
opened his business in 1905 at Water and Beekman
Streets near the old Fulton Fish Market. Early
clients included the renowned firm McKim, Mead
& White, who placed the distinctive ladders, which
glide on wheels, in the wood-paneled libraries they
designed in some of the city's finest homes. The ladders also became fixtures in the stockrooms and on
the sales floors of other businesses that, like Putnam,

would survive into the twenty-first century—
Hammacher Schlemmer (p. 83), Brooks Brothers
(p. 66), Lord & Taylor (p. 69)—along with scores of
lesser-known shoe stores, pharmacies, groceries, and
notions shops.

Putnam moved the business to Howard Street,
one block north of Canal, during the Great
Depression. Upon his retirement in 1946, he left the
company to a longtime employee, Caroline Rehm,
whose nephew, Warren Monsees, took over in 1950.
Monsees and his son, Gregg, have now been at it
longer than the founder himself. The ladders—
fashioned from oak, cherry, walnut, maple, ash, teak,
or Honduras mahogany—can be stained more than
a dozen shades, with black, brass, chrome, pewter,
nickel, gold dust, or copper hardware finishes. In
addition to the rolling ladders, the company offers
library steps, pulpit ladders, tapered window washers'
ladders, step stools, and extension trestle ladders in
heights ranging from 12 inches to 40 feet. Putnam
also preserves some of its oldest models at the shop,
ladders reclaimed from the now-defunct businesses
they have outlived.

GEORGE TAYLOR SPECIALTIES

76 FRANKLIN STREET (CHURCH-BROADWAY)
☎ (212) 226-5369　🚋 FRANKLIN ST (1/2)
MON-WED: 7:30AM-5PM; THUR: 7:30AM-6:30PM
FRI: 7:30AM-4PM

✦

THE FAMILY THAT OWNS THE BUSINESS HE FOUNDED KNOWS LITTLE OF THE LIFE OF George Taylor. They know he was a Scotsman. They know he opened a machine shop on Water Street in 1869. And they know he was the published author of at least one book of poetry. (His *The Story of Glencoe and Other Poems,* copyright 1908, sometimes turns up at rare-book shops.) The machine shop, perhaps reflecting its founder's wide range of interests, made and sold whatever metal products were in demand at the time, from buggy parts to candle snuffers.

When Chris Christou became one of the shop's three employees in 1945, its product line ranged from decorative fountains to equipment for testing the viscosity of oil. Christou wasn't there long before the owner, an elderly nephew of George Taylor, announced his retirement, selling the business — still located in its original quarters — to his staff. Christou in turn eventually bought out his two older partners and took over the business.

In the 1950s the firm acquired a company that made and sold plumbing supplies, including the "bubblers," or drinking fountains, for all the parks in the city. By the time Christou had brought his children into the business, in the 1980s, George Taylor Specialties had redefined itself as a high-end plumbing supplier. Today, Taylor stocks the lines of many makers of faucets, sinks, and accessories. If they don't stock it, they'll get it for you. And if they can't get it, they'll make it: they still have a machine shop on the premises, capable of fabricating anything from a nut or screw to an exact copy of an antique faucet — for which they carry vintage porcelain handles. They can fix anything that water runs through. And they still exclusively supply all of New York City's park bubblers.

B. WANKEL HARDWARE

1573 THIRD AVENUE (88TH-89TH STREETS)
☎ (212) 369-1200   🚊 86TH ST (4/5/6)
MON–SAT: 9:30AM–6PM; SUN: 9:30AM–5PM

✦

PLAIN WOODEN BUCKETS WERE THE BEST-
SELLING ITEM IN THE EARLY DAYS OF A
hardware store located in the heart of Yorkville. Back
when beer flowed like water, many a thirsty laborer
brought home his brew in a pail from a nearby saloon
or from one of several big breweries in the largely
German neighborhood. (At the turn of the century,
local resident Harpo Marx learned to tell time on a
brewery clock after his brother swiped his watch.)

Second-generation German-Americans Bernhart
and Elizabeth Wankel bought a building just a block
away from a Third Avenue El stop and opened their
hardware store in 1896. As Bernhart was a street
musician, tending to the business—and providing
security for her family—fell largely to Elizabeth. It
is still flourishing in the same location, now managed by the founders' great-granddaughter, the
third Wankel woman to run the company. (The late
Dr. Felix Wankel, inventor of the rotary engine, was
a relative.) In addition to beer buckets, the store's
stock at first consisted mainly of tools and materials

for the construction trade. No longer. Today the El is gone, the breweries are gone, the German restaurants are gone, scores of high-rise apartment buildings dot the landscape...and Wankel's has changed with the neighborhood. Only a small percentage of its sales are now to construction professionals. Most of its customers are Yorkville neighbors who appreciate the store's neat organization, its attentive service, and its many well-stocked departments, including automotive, garden, small appliances, pet supplies, office supplies, doors and windows, electrical, plumbing, and building supplies.

Something else that endears the store to its customers is its employment policy. Wankel's hires the physically or mentally challenged, the formerly homeless or incarcerated, runaway teens who are trying to turn their lives around, as well as refugees from war, famine, and political repression.

HENRY WESTPFAL & CO.

107 WEST 30TH STREET

(SIXTH-SEVENTH AVENUES)

☎ (212) 563-5990

🚇 34TH ST/HERALD SQ (B/D/F/N/Q/R/V/W)

MON-FRI: 9AM-6PM

✦

DISEMBARKING AT CASTLE CLINTON NEAR THE FOOT OF BROADWAY—DECADES BEFORE immigrants were processed at Ellis Island— Frederick Westpfal arrived from Westphalia in 1864. The 13-year-old immediately began training beside his father in the German cutlery industry in the Kleindeutschland section of the Lower East Side. A mere 12 years later, Frederick was able to open his own shop at 186 East Houston Street, where he earned a reputation as both a master sharpener and a skilled manufacturer of fine knives and other tools.

Westpfal's son, Frederick Jr., and his grandsons, Henry and Harold, all entered the business, which after more than 50 years moved to 32nd Street just off Fifth Avenue at the start of the Depression. The corner was the center of the now-vanished handbag manufacturing district, and selling, repairing, and sharpening the tools of its mainly Jewish craftsmen became the mainstay of Westpfal's business. After another 60 years, the company moved to 105 West 30th Street, and in 2002 it moved to its current location just next door.

Henry's nephew, Frank Schmidt, is now the owner, with the business managed by Cam Wiegmann, an employee who has sat at the same rolltop desk for the last 50 years. Leatherworking tools are still an important part of the stock at Westpfal, as are bookbinding tools, fabric shears, and other items essential to the needle trades, cooks' knives, pocketknives, and all manner of scissors, including the largest stock of hard-to-find left-handed models in the city. An oversized pair of antique shears that has been used by various New York mayors, governors, and other notables at ribbon-cutting ceremonies is available for rental. Westpfal no longer does any manufacturing, although the anvil from the old forge is still in the basement.

The company's sharpening services are its most valued contribution nowadays. Once Westpfal was one of many members of the grinders guild. Today, it is the sole survivor, and the master grinder at work on the main rig, stamped with the date 1879, has no apprentices in training. He sharpens scissors—for manicurists, hairdressers, tailors, and others—the old-fashioned way, with running water. But Westpfal's most exacting customers—the distinguished chefs of Jean-Georges, Lutèce, and Gramercy Tavern, among other top restaurants—worry that this essential service will disappear in New York if this venerable old company should ever go out of business.

IN BRIEF

BESHAR'S CARPET, 1513 FIRST AVENUE. In 1898, a newly arrived family of Armenian silk merchants began importing fine rugs from the Near East. The third generation of Beshars now offers antique and semi-antique rugs, along with antique Japanese cloisonné, Chinese porcelain, carved ivory figurines, and English and American antique furniture.

P.C. RICHARD & SON, LOCATIONS THROUGHOUT NEW YORK CITY AND THE METROPOLITAN AREA. Around the turn of the century, milkman Peter Christiaan Richard worked as a handyman for customers along his delivery route. In 1909 the Dutch immigrant opened a hardware store in Bensonhurst, Brooklyn, that evolved into the appliance chain run today by third- and fourth-generation family members.

CHARLES P. ROGERS, 55 WEST 17TH STREET. The iron and brass beds manufactured and sold today are hand-forged using the same methods and materials the company has employed since its founding in 1855.

ITALIAN RESTAURANTS

✦

BAMONTE'S RESTAURANT

32 WITHERS STREET (UNION-LORIMER STREETS)
GREENPOINT, BROOKLYN
☎ (718) 384-8831
🚇 LORIMER ST (L); METROPOLITAN AVE (G)
WED-MON: NOON-10PM

✦

ALTHOUGH PLAQUES ON THE WALL COM-
MEMORATE BOTH BAMONTE'S GOLDEN
jubilee in 1950 and the diamond in 1975, there was
no significant celebration of the 100th anniversary
in 2000. The third-generation owner didn't want to
risk omitting any of the many longtime customers
from the guest list.

The restaurant has been a family-run neighborhood place since Pasquale Bamonte—a piano
maker from a small town near Salerno, who arrived
in New York in the late 1890s—opened it as the
very-patriotic-sounding Liberty Hall. Another relative operated a cooperage next door, and one of the
many family photographs on the walls, taken in the
1940s in front of the small wood-frame house,
shows a brightly decorated Christmas tree in one of
its barrels. The restaurant offered free check cashing
at the bar, and became the smoke-filled gathering
spot for local politicians from the Italian American

Democratic League. In the 1950s, the place became one of the first in the city to take down the wall between kitchen and dining room, a generation before high-style designers of the 1980s made this a New York restaurant cliché. Yankees and Dodgers memorabilia are reminders of a time when Bamonte's was also a hangout for Italian-American ballplayers like Joe DiMaggio, Carl Furillo, and Tommy Lasorda.

Regulars and new customers today come for the comfortable, low-key ambience and to dine on starters such as grilled portobello mushrooms, anchovies with pimento, zuppa di clams, fried zucchini, and broccoli salad; for main dishes, there are many pasta selections, broiled halibut, shrimp scampi, lamb chops, steak pizzaioli, pork chops with hot or sweet vinegar peppers, plus eight veal and six chicken dishes. Desserts include tiramisu, tartufo, tortoni, spumoni, and fresh fruit in season.

As demand for barrels declined, the family real-ized the cooperage could be better used as a parking lot for customers' cars.

BARBETTA

321 WEST 46TH STREET

(EIGHTH-NINTH AVENUES)

☎ (212) 246-9171

🚇 42ND ST/PORT AUTHORITY (A/C/E)

DAILY: NOON-2:30PM, 5PM-MIDNIGHT

✦

NEWCOMERS ARE OFTEN CRESTFALLEN WHEN THEY LEARN THEY'LL BE SITTING upstairs at Barbetta instead of the grand main-floor dining room. What regulars know is that the stunning, painstakingly restored parlor rooms of Barbetta's nineteenth-century townhouses are among the city's most charming places to dine.

The restaurant, founded in 1906 by Sebastiano Maioglio, and named after his brother's goatee, was originally located near the old Metropolitan Opera House at Broadway and 39th Street. Maioglio, 26 and recently arrived from Turin, was hoping to make a living providing unpretentious Italian food in a friendly environment — while spending as much time as possible at the opera. The plan succeeded well enough that by 1925 he was able to purchase from the Astor family four noble brownstones on West 46th Street. Barbetta's move into those buildings helped establish the block as New York's Restaurant Row.

In the early 1960s, the aging founder's only daughter announced that no one but she was going to take responsibility for the family restaurant. After her father passed on, Laura Maioglio, a young art historian, applied her expertise to transform Barbetta into the dining palazzo it is today. First she purged all traces of rusticity — the checked tablecloths, the candles in Chianti bottles — in favor of sophisticated furnishings. Then she upgraded the fare, aiming to serve the finest Piedmontese cuisine in the United States.

The menu specializes in seasonal dishes prepared with white truffles unearthed by Barbetta's own truffle hounds at the family's ancestral home in Piedmont. Signature main courses — indicated on the menu with the year they were introduced — include beef braised in red wine with polenta; roasted organic rabbit in a white wine and lemon sauce with cabbage; and bolliti misti, mixed meats and broth, which must be ordered at least 48 hours ahead. Fresh game may include squab, wild hare, and venison. There is an impressive pasta range, including a number of specialties such as gnochetti ai formaggi. The dessert cart is always laden, and the award-winning wine list is among the city's best — and one of the few that includes a reserve of single-estate "super Tuscans."

FERDINANDO'S FOCACCERIA

151 UNION STREET (HICKS-COLUMBIA STREETS)
CARROLL GARDENS, BROOKLYN
☎ (718) 855-1545 🚈 CARROLL ST (F/G)
MON-THUR: 11AM-6PM; FRI-SAT: 11AM-9PM
CASH ONLY

✦

RED HOOK IS A PART OF BROOKLYN RICH IN AMERICAN HISTORY. THE NAME DATES back as far as Dutch times — the Roode Hoek being a point of land that was known for either its red-colored soil or its cranberry bogs. The area got its start as home to a great port in 1825 with the shipping boom that was spurred by the opening of the Erie Canal. Some of the stolid brick warehouses that were constructed along its wharves were requisitioned during the Civil War as supply depots, military hospitals, and prisoner-of-war camps. By the turn of the century, thousands of Irish and Italian immigrants put down roots in the area, some finding work on the busy docks, while others started ethnic specialty shops along Union and Columbia Streets to serve the neighborhood's new inhabitants.

In 1904, Ferdinando's Focacceria opened in a Union Street storefront just three blocks from the waterfront, specializing in the little sandwiches that were sold by street vendors in the open-air markets of Sicily. For decades, the restaurant served up this Sicilian comfort food even as Red Hook began to decline along with the local shipping industry. Despite the intrusion of the Brooklyn-Queens Expressway in the 1950s, a devastating blow to the neighborhood that isolated the shops from their customers, Ferdinando's remained in business.

Today, Frank Buffa, only the fourth owner of the focacceria, tends the place he inherited from his father-in-law. A little old country, a little old New York, Ferdinando's is a beautifully preserved gem, with its vintage tile floor, pressed-tin ceiling, and marble-topped tables. Loyal customers from all over the city return time and again for those sandwiches — panelle, a fried chickpea flour patty layered with ricotta cheese, or, for the more adventurous, vesteddi, made with calves' spleen — among many delicious Sicilian dishes. Other house specialties include: frutti di mare, fresh assorted seafood dressed in lemon and olive oil; arancini, rice balls stuffed with chopped meat and peas; caponatina, cold eggplant with olives, capers, and celery; pasta con sarde with sardines, fennel, and raisins; stuffed peppers; fried potato croquettes; and more.

GARGIULO'S

2911 WEST 15TH STREET (MERMAID-SURF
AVENUES), CONEY ISLAND, BROOKLYN
☎ (718) 266-4891   🚇 STILLWELL AVE (F/Q/W)
MON-SAT: NOON-10:30PM; SUN: NOON-9:30PM

✦

IN 1609 HENRY HUDSON LANDED BRIEFLY
ALONG A STRIP OF PASTORAL COASTLINE
that Dutch settlers would come to name for the
abundance of rabbits, the konijn, that lived there.
Two centuries later, Walt Whitman loved swimming
in its "pure, sparkling sea-water." Its exclusive hotels
drew the elite of Civil War-era society. By the 1890s,
it was office clerks, shop girls, and factory workers
who, with a 25-cent steamship ride, escaped the
summer heat of the city streets to splash in the
waves, thrill to the amusement park rides (the first
roller coaster opened in 1884, the Ferris wheel a
decade later), and sample the resort's most popular
food treat (the frankfurter, introduced in 1870). By
the early twentieth century, Coney Island had
become a gaudy, glitzy, raucous pleasure precinct
known throughout the world.

Among the first year-round residents were
Italian families like the Gargiulos of Sorento, who
opened a restaurant on Mermaid Avenue in 1907,

almost a decade before the legendary Nathan's set up shop a block away. Louis Gargiulo's became one of the anchors of the Italian enclave; rumor has it that the young Al Capone worked here as a busboy. Having outgrown the premises, the restaurant moved around the corner to a converted stable in the 1920s, where it has remained ever since.

The family, which barely held on to the business through the Depression, sold the place in 1965 to the Russo brothers — Michael, Victor, and Nino — whose offspring, a veritable army of cousins, now operate the eatery alongside a catering business. On any given weekend, several weddings, confirmations, bridal showers, and other private affairs are celebrated simultaneously in the various banquet rooms. The large menu includes starters such as pimentos and anchovies, fish salad, mozzarella in carrozza and fried artichokes. Pasta specialties, include gnocchi, manicotti, perciatelli putanesca, linguini with pesto, spaghetti ten different ways, and the distinctive dish of the house, fusili with artichoke sauce. Sausage and peppers, pork chops pizzaiola, a dozen veal preparations, nine chicken dishes, lobster, shrimp, calamari, scungilli, and red snapper are among the main dishes. Desserts include spumoni, tortoni, tartufo, and zabaglione over fresh berries.

JOHN'S OF 12TH STREET

302 EAST 12TH STREET

(FIRST-SECOND AVENUES)

☎ (212) 475-9531   🚇 1ST AVE (L)

🚇 14TH ST/UNION SQ (4/5/6/N/Q/R/W)

MON-SAT: 4PM-11PM; SUN: 3:30PM-10:30PM

CASH ONLY

✦

THE ELABORATE 1880S-VINTAGE TILE FLOOR AT JOHN'S RESTAURANT MUST BE one of the most beautiful in New York City. The owners—only the third in the restaurant's history—lovingly maintain it, washing and bleaching it daily. However, they have never attempted to repair the missing patch of tiles in the middle of the room. When they bought the place in 1972, they were warned by the sellers that the floor might not withstand the work; the hole has been there for more than 60 years.

John Pucciatti, who came from a small town in Umbria, started the restaurant here in 1908 at a time when there was no East Village, just the Lower East Side. The neighborhood was a classic New York melting pot with Italians on First Avenue, Jews on Second, Germans around Tompkins Square Park; for a time Butch Cassidy and the Sundance Kid lived in a rooming house down the block. Pucciatti had the Belgian mosaic wainscoting brought over from Europe and paid a local artist in free meals for the paintings that hang on the walls; the breakfront and the mirrors that line the room are also original.

The General Electric refrigerator that now chills beer and wine dates from 1919, the year Prohibition was enacted. Through the '20s, drinkers were sent via a hidden staircase to the less conspicuous family quarters upstairs. Business boomed, and the street was lined with the Packards and Dusenbergs of visiting revelers seeking bootleg booze. Nonetheless, Pucciatti was thrilled to be legal again when Repeal was announced. To celebrate, he ceremoniously lit a candle, and continued to do so every evening for years to come, a tradition maintained to this day at the wax-laden shrine in the back dining room.

Tradition is also observed in the kitchen, which still does all its own butchering and baking. The chef has been there for more than 30 years and was trained by the chef before him. The bill of fare is classic old-style Italian. Starters include roasted peppers and anchovies, stuffed mushrooms, and baked clams arreganata. Among the many entrées are sausages broiled with peppers and veal sweetbreads with mushrooms. The seafood list includes at least three preparations of calamari, shrimp parmigiana, and pasta with white or red clam sauce.

LANZA RESTAURANT

168 FIRST AVENUE (10TH-11TH STREETS)
☎ (212) 674-7014   🚇 ASTOR PL (6); 1ST AVE (L)
MON-SAT: NOON-11PM; SUN: NOON-10PM

✦

MICHELE LANZA, OF NAPLES, WAS A CHEF TO NO LESS THAN VICTOR EMMANUEL OF Italy, but he aspired to open his own restaurant in America. With the king's blessing he crossed the Atlantic and, around 1902, opened a tiny eatery in the Italian section that was just beginning to establish itself on First Avenue near Tenth Street. In 1904 he opened a full-fledged dining establishment on the same block.

It was, and still is, a family place, not only for its customers but for the three generations of Lanzas who ran it. Although they sold their interest in the mid-1990s (preferring to focus on their successful funeral-home business elsewhere in the neighborhood), their portraits still line the walls — a symbol of current owner Anthony Macagnone's commitment to maintaining the Lanza tradition. The menu includes such classics as prosciutto with sweet melon, sliced mozzarella and tomatoes, fried calamari, veal parmigiana or scaloppine, linguine with fresh clams in oil and garlic, trout with garlic and rosemary, chicken breast parmigiana, and a Caesar salad. In addition to its standard à la carte bill of fare, Lanza has three prix-fixe menus—for lunch, early dinner, and a late-night pasta dinner.

From the stained glass and neon signs of its façade to its pressed-tin ceiling, hand-painted murals, open kitchen, and cozy dining room, Lanza has remained true to itself—an authentic Italian-American landmark that has endured for a century despite the unruly, constantly changing neighborhood just outside its door.

LUNA RESTAURANT

112 MULBERRY STREET

(CANAL-HESTER STREETS)

☎ (212) 226-8657

🚇 CANAL ST (6/J/M/N/Q/R/W/Z)

SUN-THUR: NOON-MIDNIGHT

FRI-SAT: NOON-2AM

✦

THE WOMEN WHO RUN LUNA TODAY AREN'T REALLY SURE WHEN THE RESTAURANT first opened for business. They know that Alberta Manna started cooking up pasta in a basement on Mulberry Street for other Neapolitans in turn-of-the-century Little Italy. It was not a big deal; it was simply what she did to make a living. It probably never occurred to her that a century later anyone would want to know.

After a few years Alberta took over a street-level storefront two doors down, where her family still prepares her recipes today. Unlike so many of the old restaurants in Little Italy that have obliterated all traces of their early days with slick, modern decor, Luna looks like a place that has simply evolved over many decades of additions and subtractions—an old breakfront here, a new Venus de Milo there. If any one time period asserts itself more strongly than the others, however, it must be the 1950s, when the family expanded into the adjoining storefront. Customers dine at tables covered with colorful, vintage-style vinyl cloths while Italian doo-wop music plays in the background. In the back room, simply rendered murals of the Bay of Naples and other landmarks of southern Italy adorn the walls.

Luna's prices exist in something of a time warp as well, making this one of the least expensive restaurants in the neighborhood, and sharing the extra-large portions is encouraged. The menu advises: "Speak up when Vegetarian," and there are many no-meat options among the pasta dishes. There are a dozen veal preparations, chicken cacciatore, lobster, shrimp, clams, and calamari.

MANGANARO'S

488 NINTH AVENUE (37TH-38TH STREETS)
☎ (212) 563-5331
🚇 42ND ST/PORT AUTHORITY (A/C/E)
MON-FRI: 8AM-7PM; SAT: 9AM-7PM

✦

WHEN JAMES MANGANARO CAME HOME FROM SERVING IN THE FIRST WORLD War, he returned to the simple Italian groceria he had opened in Hell's Kitchen in 1910. When Prohibition shuttered his aunt's and uncle's nearby wine and liquors store, which they had run since 1893, he moved his business into their location.

Despite the fact that this was a rough immigrant neighborhood, the store became a popular gathering spot for homesick Italian performers from the nearby Metropolitan Opera House. The place today is not all that different. The original, turn-of-the-century interior is maintained by James Manganaro's grandson, Sal Dell'Orto, and several of Sal's five daughters. Their loyal customers line up, cafeteria-style, at the rear counter to order sausage and peppers, pasta—with meat sauce, marinara, pesto, red or white clam sauce—gnocchi, polenta, rice balls, veal, chicken, or eggplant parmigiana, fried calamari, caponata, marinated mushrooms, and seafood salad. All the standard hero ingredients are available, along with less traditional additions such as smoked chicken, brie, and arugula. Up front, boxes of pasta, olive oils, vinegars, and other imported Italian specialty foods are for sale beside the busy espresso bar and pastry case.

Another member of the Manganaro family runs the much newer and slicker Italian sandwich shop and restaurant next door.

MONTE'S

451 CARROLL STREET
(THIRD AVENUE-NEVINS STREET),
SOUTH BROOKLYN
☎ (718) 624-8984
🚇 UNION ST (M/N/R); CARROLL ST (F/G)
MON-FRI: NOON-10PM; SAT: 4PM-11PM
SUN: 2PM-10PM

✦

ALTHOUGH THE FOUNDING BROTHERS, NICK AND ANGELO MONTEMORENO, WERE FROM the area around Naples, and the cuisine served here has always been southern Italian, the charming murals that line Monte's dining room depict Venice. Perhaps this is a sly nod to the Gowanus Canal, the mid-nineteenth century waterway just up the block. (The tiny Carroll Street Bridge over the canal dates from 1889 and is the oldest retractile bridge in the United States.) In 1906, however, there were no murals, just the mahogany-topped oak bar from which the family — with the newly abbreviated name Monte — began serving their South Brooklyn neighbors. The Venetian canal scenes and the fish tanks behind the bar were added in the 1930s when the restaurant was enlarged to become something of a small-scale Italian cabaret, whose size did not discourage such headliners as Frank Sinatra and Sammy Davis Jr. from performing here. And it is here that the 1955 Brooklyn Dodgers celebrated their World Series victory. Today there's still a little fold-away stage for the occasional singer.

The house specialties include roasted peppers and anchovies, clams oreganata, mussels in white wine, and pastas — primavera, Bolognese, manicotti, and paglia e fieno ("straw and hay," green and white noodles in a cream sauce with fresh mushrooms) among others. Pork chops pizzaiola, veal (scallopine, marsala, parmigiano, and six other ways), and, not listed on the menu but available for those who know, giambotta (boneless chicken breast, sausage, mushroom, onion, potatoes, sweet and hot peppers sautéed in white wine and topped with strips of filet mignon) are main dish options. Seafood choices include fried calamari, frutti di mare, and in honor of the murals, shrimp gondolier, with black olives and prosciutto in marinara sauce.

RAO'S

455 EAST 114TH STREET (PLEASANT AVENUE)
☎ (212) 722-6709　🚇 116TH ST (6)
MON-FRI: 6PM-11PM　　CASH ONLY

✦

WHEN VINCENT RAO AND HIS BROTHER
LOUIS TOOK OVER THEIR FAMILY'S BAR
during the Depression, they could not have imagined
that the place known in the neighborhood as "The
Hole"—because the entrance was several steps down
from the pavement—would come to have the most
sought-after tables in the city.

Their father, Charles Rao, had arrived as a child
from a small town near Naples to the predominantly
Italian section of East Harlem in the 1880s. The
colorful neighborhood was also home to immigrants
from Ireland and Germany—Groucho Marx was
born down the street in 1890—and the noisy, crowded
streets were lined with their various pushcarts, ethnic
markets, and gathering spots. In 1896, Rao purchased
one of the area's many corner saloons, one that distinguished itself with fine pewter pipes that delivered
beer from the wooden casks in the basement to the
taps at the bar. Following Charles' untimely death
in 1909, his brother Joseph took over, keeping the
bar open through the years of Prohibition, when

wine made in a neighbor's cellar was pumped into Rao's through a hose.

After Repeal, the family turned the saloon into a proper restaurant, a neighborhood place that has long outlasted its original neighbors. Even as most of the Italian families moved away and the area began to decline, Rao's held firm. In addition to its longtime regulars, who came back to East Harlem just to eat here, the restaurant became a cult favorite of many who were drawn by the superb old-style Italian food and comforting old-style décor: the year-round Christmas lights, the figure of the Madonna in the window, the warm, dark woods of the paneling, the booths, and the bar. Because each of the eight tables is booked in perpetuity by the regulars, it is legendarily difficult to secure a seat.

No menu is brought to the lucky few who assemble in the small dining room. The waiter simply pulls up a chair and says what's good that night — mozzarella in carrozza, orecchiette with broccoli rabe and sausage, spaghetti alla puttanesca, risotto Milanese, swordfish Livornese, veal marsala, steak pizzaiola, or the famous lemon chicken. For dessert, there's espresso with tiramisu, amaretti, or biscotti. Those who can't get a table can content themselves with Rao's bottled sauces, roasted peppers, and line of artisanal pastas, sold in gourmet shops throughout the country.

VINCENT'S CLAM BAR

119 MOTT STREET (HESTER STREET)
☎ (212) 226-8133
🚇 CANAL ST (6/J/M/N/Q/R/W/Z)
SUN-THUR: 11:30AM-1:30AM
FRI-SAT: 11:30AM-3AM

✦

NOT ONLY IS IT STILL OWNED BY THE FOUNDING FAMILY, VINCENT'S IS THE kind of family restaurant that seems to make family of just about everyone who ever worked there. On any given day, the former bartender—now in his 80s—will come by for a visit and perhaps take a snooze seated on one of the counter stools. Another employee, more recently retired, had been a neighborhood kid who hung out around the restaurant; "Red"—the guy who made the sauce—worked there for 56 years. One of the men in the kitchen today also grew up hanging out at Vincent's and has been on the job for almost 40 years.

Sicilian newcomers in America, Giuseppe and Carmela Siano started out in 1904 with only a sidewalk clam bar and the single storefront at the corner of Mott and Hester Streets in the heart of Little Italy. The couple named the place after their small son, Vincent. He grew along with the business, which eventually expanded down Hester Street toward Mulberry by taking over the adjoining florist's shop and pork store. The specialty, of course, was—and is—clams (steamed, baked, on the half shell, in red or white sauce) along with oysters, shrimp, scungilli, calamari, mussels, scallops, lobster, soft-shell crabs, and other seafood loved by Sicilians. Diners who prefer their pasta with meatballs, veal, chicken, or sautéed vegetables will not go hungry either.

Today, another Vincent—a cousin of the founders—oversees the restaurant's spruced-up premises, which sport a bright vintage-style tile floor and a freshly painted pressed-tin ceiling.

IN BRIEF

ANGELO OF MULBERRY STREET, 146 MULBERRY STREET. Since 1902.

LOMBARDI'S PIZZA, 32 SPRING STREET. This restaurant is the direct descendant of what may well be the first pizza parlor in the country, which opened down the block in 1905. That original location was abandoned when the persistent rumbling of the Lexington Avenue subway line ruined the precious coal-fired oven. Lombardi's still prepares pies the old-fashioned way—in a traditional coal oven.

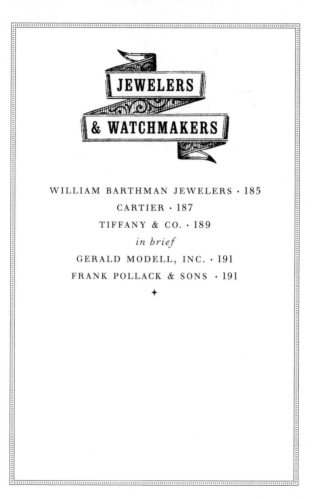

JEWELERS & WATCHMAKERS

WILLIAM BARTHMAN
JEWELERS

174 BROADWAY (MAIDEN LANE)
☎ (212) 732-0890   🚇 FULTON ST (4/5)
MON-FRI: 8AM-5:30PM

✦

THE DISPLAY WINDOWS AT WILLIAM BARTHMAN JEWELERS HAVE BEEN SHATtered twice in the store's long history. In 1911, a horse galloping out of control crashed into one of them, scattering a quarter-of-a-million dollars' worth of gemstones across busy lower Broadway. Ninety years later, the collapse of the south tower of the World Trade Center, a block away, destroyed two of the windows and the front door; the evacuated staff returned the next day uncertain whether they would find anything remaining of the historic shop, which has conducted business at this location since 1884. Luckily, the store survived; the distinctive set-into-the-pavement clock—a 1920s replacement of the turn-of-the-century original—was undamaged.

Once a part of the city's first diamond, jewelry, and watchmaking district, Barthman is now the only dealer remaining. The founder was a German-Dutch immigrant who married the daughter of a Maiden Lane jeweler before opening his own shop down the street in the early 1870s. Even after he traded up to the prime location at the corner, William Barthman knew how to be thrifty. He outfitted his new store with graceful 1869 wood-and-glass display cases that he purchased second hand. As the residential part of the city moved uptown, Barthman's former clients were replaced by robber barons, business tycoons, and gangsters. "Diamond" Jim Brady, who was rumored to own more than a million dollars worth of jewelry, was a regular customer.

The Barthman family maintained the store until one year shy of its centennial in 1984, when they sold to the current owners. Today, William's secondhand cases display glistening jewelry and a considerable selection of Rolex watches, which fly out of the store during bonus season on Wall Street.

CARTIER

✦

WHEN PIERRE CARTIER SOLD THE FAMOUSLY CURSED HOPE DIAMOND IN 1910 FOR $154,000, he inserted a clause into the sale contract stipulating that in the event of accidental death befalling any member of the buyer's immediate family within 18 months of the purchase, the company would take back the jewel as well as pay a large indemnity. The unusual transaction took place at the year-old New York branch of the prestigious jeweler, located on the fourth floor of 712 Fifth Avenue (the current site of Henri Bendel, p. 59).

Following his service in the French army during World War I, Pierre looked for a more appropriate site for the firm his grandfather, Louis-François, had founded in Paris in 1847. When Maisie Cadwell Plant, the wife of a wealthy yachtsman and financier, expressed her desire for a rare double-strand Oriental pearl Cartier necklace, the shrewd jeweler struck a deal that made everyone happy: he traded the necklace, valued at $1.2 million, for the Plant's lovely mansion at Fifth Avenue and 52nd Street.

In October 1917, Cartier opened in the Renaissance-style palace and has been there ever since. Five separate viewing salons—one each for pearls, diamonds, rubies, emeralds, and religious jewelry—allowed customers to consider their purchases in complete privacy. In addition to gems, the company fabricated exquisite timepieces (J. P. Morgan bought one of the so-called Mystery Clocks, with their baffling hidden mechanism) and wristwatches (such as the Tank, designed to honor the Allied tank crews of the Great War). Other luxury products came later, including eyewear, fragrances, engraved stationery, writing instruments, lighters, leather goods, scarves, silver, and crystal.

New York real estate being what it is, the Cartier building is now worth more than ten Plant necklaces.

Additional location: 828 Madison Avenue.

TIFFANY & CO.

727 FIFTH AVENUE (57TH STREET)
☎ (212) 755-8000
🚇 5TH AVE/59TH ST (N/R/W)
MON-FRI: 10AM-7PM; SAT: 10AM-6PM

✦

TIFFANY HAD BEEN IN BUSINESS FOR ONE SCORE AND FOUR YEARS WHEN ABRAHAM Lincoln visited the jeweler's shop at Broadway and Broome Street to buy a gift for his wife, Mary Todd, on the occasion of his first inauguration. The president selected a suite of pearls—a bracelet, earrings, necklace, and brooch. The jeweler would have wrapped the purchase in the distinctive robin's-egg blue box that the shop had introduced in 1837, its first year of operation. Mrs. Lincoln adored her Tiffany pearls and was often photographed wearing them.

New Englanders Charles Tiffany and his partner John Young had begun their enterprise near City Hall as a stationery shop, to which they added jewelry, crystal, and imported Swiss watches a few years later. When Young traveled to Paris in 1848 during one of that city's most convulsive revolutions, he was unwittingly in the right place at the right time. He managed to acquire the finest jewels of the fleeing French aristocracy, an inventory that established the reputation the firm has maintained up to today. Just five years later, Young sold out his interest to Tiffany, who was taking the company into the design and sale of commemorative silver objects, a business that expanded during the Civil War to include swords, flags, and even surgical instruments for the Union Army.

In the booming post-war economy, Tiffany moved to Union Square in the company of other exclusive shops such as Brooks Brothers (p. 66), FAO Schwarz (p. 91), Steinway & Sons (p. 325), and Dempsey & Carroll, the stationer-engravers (p. 289). While at this location, Charles' son, Louis Comfort Tiffany, the renowned decorative-arts designer, joined the firm, which now sold his jewelry and enamels. Another move in 1905 to a Venetian-style palazzo designed by McKim, Mead & White at 37th Street and Fifth established the avenue's reputation as the city's new preeminent shopping district.

Transporting more than ten million dollars' worth of gems one mile up the avenue to the current location made headlines in 1940. The façade of the 57th Street building incorporates the so-called Atlas clock, which had originally been mounted in 1853 over the store's entrance on lower Broadway. The grand main floor, which today draws tourists from all over the world, encompasses more than

8,000 square feet and features a concealed lighting system that allows the jewels—displayed in sleek cherry wood-and-glass showcases—to be viewed to their best advantage.

Tiffany is also a leading seller of watches, clocks, sterling silver, china, glassware, flatware, and true to its origins, engraved stationery.

IN BRIEF

GERALD MODELL, INC. TWO LOCATIONS IN MANHATTAN, TWO IN BROOKLYN. New York's leading collateral loan brokers—pawnshops—are descendants, along with Modell's sporting goods empire (p. 89), of the same Lower West Side push-cart business of the 1880s.

FRANK POLLACK & SONS, 608 FIFTH AVENUE. A potential customer must be recommended by a current client to make an appointment with this private jewelry designer, which has been a family business since 1905.

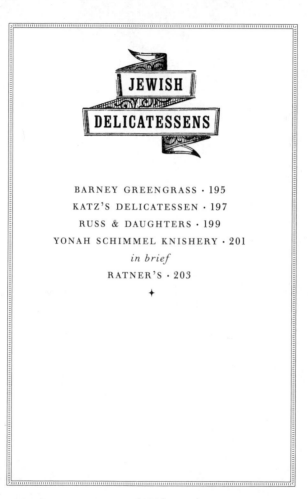

JEWISH DELICATESSENS

✦

BARNEY GREENGRASS

541 AMSTERDAM AVENUE (86TH-87TH STREETS)

☎ (212) 724-4707   🚇 86TH ST (1/2/B/C)

STORE: TUE-SUN: 8AM-6PM

RESTAURANT: TUE-FRI: 8:30AM-4PM

SAT-SUN: 8:30AM-5PM

✦

WELL INTO THE NINETEENTH CENTURY, THE TRACTS OF FARMS AND COUNTRY estates covering what is now the Upper West Side were known as Bloomingdale Village. In his Knickerbocker's History of New York, Washington Irving described the area as "a sweet rural valley, beautiful with many a bright flower, refreshed by many a pure streamlet, and enlivened here and there by a delectable little Dutch cottage." Edgar Allan Poe and his wife, seeking to escape the "insufferably dirty" streets of the city, moved in 1844 to a 200-acre working farm near today's Broadway and 84th Street.

A visit to Barney Greengrass on a weekend morning will settle any questions as to whether or not the Upper West Side is still a rustic, pastoral part of town. The Formica wainscoting, the fluorescent lights, the vinyl seats, the showcase displaying a tempting array of smoked fish, and the ravenous throng proclaim that civilization arrived here a long time ago.

Barney Greengrass, who learned the trade on the Lower East Side, opened an appetizing store — that is, a Jewish delicatessen — in Harlem in 1908 and moved the business down to the present location two decades later. An early fan dubbed Greengrass the "Sturgeon King," a moniker emblazoned on the storefront to this day. Barney's son, Moe, grew up in the business and later took over; Moe's son, Gary, followed a similar path — which brings the story up to date.

The fish list includes sturgeon, of course, several variations on smoked salmon — none less than transcendent — gravlax, kippered salmon, whitefish, sable, pickled herring, smoked rainbow brook trout, the three varieties of Russian caviar, and fresh salmon roe. There's corned beef, pastrami, turkey, salami, chopped liver, and various fish salads; bagels and bialys; plain and fancy cream cheeses; homemade borscht and a fine matzoh ball soup. Rugelach, babka, and halvah complete the meal.

KATZ'S DELICATESSEN

205 EAST HOUSTON STREET (LUDLOW STREET)
☎ (212) 254-2246 🚊 2ND AVE (F/V)
SUN-THUR: 8AM-10PM; FRI-SAT: 8AM-3AM
CASH ONLY

✦

THE LITERAL-MINDED SIGN PAINTER HIRED
BY KATZ'S DELICATESSEN INQUIRED WHAT
exactly the owners wanted on the billboard outside
their place. "Katz's, that's all," was the simple response.
"Katz's. That's All" has greeted visitors to this Lower
East Side institution for decades. Low-level confusion
continues inside the bright, loud, cafeteria-style
restaurant, where baffled first-timers are handed a
ticket (it will be scribbled on by the servers to indicate
to the cashier what you ate) and then confronted by
two identical sets of Formica tables (only those
against the wall are served by waiters). Those who opt
to order directly from the countermen will join a
seemingly formless, lawless line and then stake out
one of the self-serve tables. Once seated, both groups
will dig into some of the best delicatessen in the city
—the city with the best delicatessen in the world.

It's been like this at Katz's —minus the Formica,
the fluorescent lights, the refrigerated soda cases—
since 1888, when the Iceland brothers started the

business. Willy Katz, a recent immigrant, entered the partnership in 1903, and was joined several years later by his brother, Benny, to buy out the founders. Actors, singers, and comedians from the thriving Yiddish theater district along Second Avenue filled the restaurant. In those days, Katz's was one of several dozen kosher delis in the lively, crowded neighborhood; today it is one of a few survivors.

Although turkey and roast beef have been added to the more traditional pastrami, corned beef, and tongue, everything — the meats, the pickles (new pickles, sours, half-sours, pickled tomatoes), even the mustard — is all still made by hand on the premises. Salamis — responsible for spawning Katz's slogan "Send a Salami to Your Boy in the Army" during World War II — are hung from the ceiling above the takeout counter, where you can also buy lengths of frankfurters, garlicky knobwurst, coleslaw, potato salad, and anything else on the menu to go.

In addition to introducing many generations of Americans from around the country and immigrants from all over the world to New York deli, Katz's has also served four sitting U.S. presidents — FDR, Jimmy Carter, Ronald Reagan, and Bill Clinton, whose legendary appetite took on two hot dogs, a pastrami sandwich, and french fries.

RUSS & DAUGHTERS

179 EAST HOUSTON STREET
(ALLEN-ORCHARD STREETS)
☎ (212) 475-4880   🚇 2ND AVE (F/V)
MON-SAT: 9AM-7PM; SUN: 8AM-5:30PM

✦

LIKE MANY OF THE EASTERN EUROPEAN JEWS WHO EMIGRATED TO NEW YORK IN the last decades of the nineteenth century, Joel Russ had a prodigious work ethic. He was also irascible and impatient. Having learned the herring business from his sister, he began working the streets in 1900 with a horse and wagon, making deliveries throughout the Lower East Side. He and his wife, Bella, took on an Orchard Street storefront in 1914 before moving around the corner to the present location in the 1920s.

Russ's ill temper was famous in the neighborhood. If a customer asked the wrong question or seemed too picky, the explosive proprietor, shouting in Yiddish, promptly threw the offender out of the store. The business limped along until Russ discovered that when his three pretty, personable daughters — Hattie, Ida, and Anne — took over behind the counter, both he and the customers were much happier. The girls didn't do too badly either, each meeting her future husband through the business.

In the beginning, the stock was limited to schmaltz herring in a barrel, pickles in a barrel, and salt-cured lox. Now in the hands of Anne's son, Mark, and his family, there is far more to choose from. In addition to the original smoked fish offerings, there are whitefish, sable, sturgeon, Scandinavian-style herring fillets (in mustard-dill sauce or lemon-ginger sauce), Swedish matjes herring, Icelandic schmaltz fillets, German roll-mops, Holland herring, Scottish salmon, wild Pacific king salmon, Gaspé salmon, gravlax, and salmon tartare. Salads include tuna, egg, whitefish, eggplant, and herring with beets and apples. People from all over the city come to Russ & Daughters for their well priced beluga, osetra, and sevruga caviar, as well as for Alaskan salmon, American sturgeon, and flying fish roe. Nuts, dried fruits, halvah, chocolates, and coffees take up a second counter.

YONAH SCHIMMEL KNISHERY

137 EAST HOUSTON STREET
(FORSYTHE-ELDRIDGE STREETS)
☏ (212) 477-2858 🚇 2ND AVE (F/V)
DAILY: 9AM-7PM

✦

TAPED TO THE WALLS OF YONAH SCHIM-MEL'S ARE FADING PHOTOGRAPHS OF THE neighborhood and tattered magazine articles that date from a time when most Americans had to be told what a knish was. Among them is a yellowed newspaper clipping about a man who came in one day and anxiously inquired if the store's dumbwaiter was still in use and could he see it. Assured that it was, he lovingly ran his fingers over every inch of its frame. Through his tears he explained to the baffled owner of the shop that his earliest recollection was being brought to Schimmel's as a child shortly before his immigrant parents had to return to Europe, leaving him in the care of a relative. They never came back, victims of the Holocaust. His only memory of his mother and father was standing with them in front of the Schimmel dumbwaiter.

There are many stories at this legendary knishery, none more important than that of Yonah Schimmel himself. The newly arrived rabbi from

Eastern Europe couldn't support himself on the money he earned teaching at a Hebrew school. He turned to baking knishes to supplement his income, selling them for years in the street from a pushcart. By 1910 he was successful enough to open a storefront on Houston Street, where his children and grandchildren have worked ever since.

A photograph of Yonah Schimmel in the window greets customers who line up for takeout or to sit at one of the long, narrow Formica tables that fill the simple dining room. Although croissants and mineral waters have been added to the menu, it is still the knishes — handmade with no preservatives or additives, baked not fried — that draw the faithful here. Brought up from the basement ovens in that old dumbwaiter, they are filled with potato, kasha, red cabbage, mushroom, spinach, broccoli, vegetable, or sweet potato. Blintzes, borsht — served by the glass — apple strudel, rugalah, poppy seed cake, and homemade yogurt round out the traditional offerings. Soda, lemonade, and egg creams — chocolate, vanilla, strawberry, and coffee — are the preferred beverages.

RATNER'S, 138 DELANCEY STREET. This Lower East Side restaurant, now open only on Sundays, has served kosher dairy food since 1905.

PASTA MAKERS

GROCERIAS &

GOURMET SHOPS

✦

ALLEVA DAIRY

188 GRAND STREET (MULBERRY STREET)
☎ (212) 226-7990   🚊 GRAND ST (S)
MON-SAT: 8:30AM-6PM; SUN: 8:30AM-3PM

✦

THE PAINTED VINTAGE GLASS SIGN THAT OFFERS "BURRO E UOVA" IS A VIVID reminder of a time when most of the customers at this latteria spoke only Italian. Today, as the Italian population has largely moved away from the Lower East Side, shoppers are as likely to be speaking Spanish, Chinese, or maybe even English. Butter and eggs can still be bought at Alleva, along with scores of imported Italian cheeses—scamorze, provolone, gorgonzola, ricotta salata, pecorino romano, parmigiano, and more. Prosciutto, sausages, and various Italian specialty foods are also available.

Pino Alleva emigrated to the United States from the small town of Benevento near Naples and opened her dairy business on Grand Street in 1892. During the early 1920s she moved several doors west toward Mulberry Street to the current storefront—with its simple period interior of white-tile walls and a pressed-tin ceiling—where her great-grandson, Robert Alleva, now runs what the family proudly proclaims is the oldest Italian cheese store in the nation.

Each week the miniscule shop turns out an astonishing 4,000 pounds of fresh mozzarella—smoked, salted, unsalted, seasoned bocconcini—and ricotta, all "sono fatte con puro latte," prepared with pure milk, according to Pina's time-honored recipes.

A.L. BAZZINI CO.

339 GREENWICH STREET (JAY STREET)

☎ (212) 334-1280   🚊 FRANKLIN ST (1/2)

DAILY: 7:30AM-8PM

✦

ANTHONY BAZZINI, WHO LIVED TO BE NEARLY 100 YEARS OLD, HELD ONLY ONE JOB OVER the course of his long life.

When he was still a boy, in the 1890s, his family brought him to New York from Genoa, Italy. He was still quite young when he went to work for a company —founded in 1886—that processed, packaged, and sold nuts. Around 1915, he bought the business. It has borne his name ever since, selling nuts to stores and supermarkets up and down the East Coast.

In the late 1960s the company, chased by the construction of the World Trade Center from its home near City Hall, relocated to a loft building several blocks north. A decade later the elderly Bazzini died. With no immediate heirs, the enterprise went to family member who wanted to sell the company but did not want to risk the good reputation associated with the Bazzini name.

It took a while, but they finally met the right man, Rocco Damato, a social studies teacher who also owned a restaurant and, in his spare time, ran a small wholesale-nut company. Once they found each other, the Bazzini heirs recognized that Damato had the desire and ability to do right by the business, and, in 1983, they sold him the firm.

As the neighborhood was colonized by loft dwellers and other non-industrial tenants — Robert De Niro's TriBeCa Film Center, for instance, is just a block north — it became increasingly clear that, while the site was no longer a good spot for a nut-processing plant, it was ideal for something else. In 2002, after moving its roasting, packaging, and shipping facilities to the Bronx, the company threw open the doors of its thoroughly renovated ground-floor gourmet shop. Now, in addition to an enticing selection of fresh cashews, almonds, pistachios, walnuts, and peanuts, Bazzini's offers prime meats, fish, produce, prepared foods, coffee by the pound or by the cup (to be sipped under a skylight), domestic and imported cheeses, dried fruits, housewares, bagels, muffins, cakes, and a soda fountain serving egg creams, root beer floats, and black cows.

BRUNO KING OF RAVIOLI

2204 BROADWAY (78TH-79TH STREETS)
☎ (212) 580-8150   🚇 79TH ST (1/2)
MON-FRI: 8AM-9PM; SAT-SUN: 8AM-8PM

✦

IN THE LATE 1800S, WHEN PASTA MAKER Bruno Cavalli arrived in New York from the Piedmont region of Italy, few Americans had ever seen, tasted, or even heard of ravioli. By 1905 Cavalli had set up his own storefront factory on West 27th Street and was producing ravioli for Italian immigrants, as well as adventurous eaters of every ethnicity.

Cavalli carefully packed the ravioli—in shoe boxes—and delivered it on his bicycle to the restaurants that were his primary customers. A small retail store in front of the factory catered to people who preferred to eat at home. The regulars knew that Cavalli and his wife were also busy raising a family. Right there in the factory, their infant sons, Louis and Amerigo, slept cradled in wooden macaroni crates. Business was good, and by the 1930s, when their father was ready to retire to Italy, the Cavalli boys knew the business inside-out. The retirement didn't last long, however, as Bruno was soon back with a new tortellini machine from Milan.

Today the company is in the hands of the third and fourth generations of the family, with a trio of shops in Manhattan served by a company-owned factory in New Jersey. The quality is as high as ever; the ricotta cheese that fills Bruno's most popular ravioli, for instance, has been produced by the same farm for the past 60 years. Where the original store offered a limited selection of raviolis, the current menu includes many varieties of homemade pasta and sauces, prepared pasta dishes, oils and vinegars, spices, fresh produce, and a full deli department.

Other locations: 387 Second Avenue; 249 Eighth Avenue.

DI PALO DAIRY

206 GRAND STREET (MOTT STREET)
☎ (212) 226-1033   🚋 GRAND ST (S)
MON-SAT: 9AM-6:30PM; SUN: 9AM-3PM

✦

MOST NEW YORKERS WOULD NOT IMAGINE THAT THEY COULD PURCHASE A FINE wedding present at this modest-looking cheese shop on the Lower East Side. But there among the frozen ravioli and tortellini, the olives and peppers, the prosciutto and salami, the pecorino romano and gorgonzola, the freshly made ricotta and mozzarella, are diminutive bottles of what has been called "black gold," hundred-year-old balsamic vinegars that sell for several hundred dollars.

The DiPalos, fourth generation of their family in the business in Little Italy, are passionate about their store, their heritage, and the quality and meaning of the food they have shared with their neighbors since 1910. Balsamic vinegar, they will explain, is a metaphor for relationships between people: the longer it ages, the thicker and sweeter and more complex it becomes; in the old country it was often a part of a bride's dowry, and it remains the perfect gift to bestow on two people embarking on a new life together.

Great-grandfather Saviano DiPalo first opened his latteria down the block selling fresh milk from large cans that were brought by horse-drawn carts from dairy farms in Queens and Brooklyn. For a nickel, customers bringing their own pitchers would ladle out the milk and perhaps buy some of the butter, ricotta, or mozzarella that was made on the premises. By the mid-1920s, Saviano's daughter, Conchetta, and her husband opened a branch in the 1870s-era tenement building at the corner where the business has continued ever since.

Today, customers squeeze into this extremely popular small shop, jockeying for the attention of the sales staff. In addition to the spectacular variety of imported cheeses and cured meats are coffees, preserves, breads, artisanal pastas, sauces, and olive oils from all regions of Italy that are worthy of the superior vinegars. Everyone is encouraged to sample.

RAFFETTO'S

144 WEST HOUSTON STREET
(MACDOUGAL-SULLIVAN STREETS)
☎ (212) 777-1261   🚇 HOUSTON ST (1/2)
TUE-FRI: 9AM-6:30PM; SAT: 9AM-6PM

✦

WHEN THE LARGE CHURCH OF SAINT ANTHONY OF PADUA WAS ERECTED IN 1886 on the corner of Houston and Sullivan Streets, there were so many newly arrived Italians settling in the area south of Washington Square Park that the neighborhood became known as another Little Italy. One of the newcomers in the area, a young man named Marcello Raffetto, opened a pasta shop a block from the church in 1902. Here he made the cheese-stuffed ravioli typical of Naples, as well as the ravioli filled with meat and spinach that were preferred in his native Genoa. Just four years later, he moved the shop around the corner to a more visible location on Houston Street, where he prospered enough that by the early 1920s he was able to buy the building and then comfortably retire with his wife and two young children to the Italian Riviera, leaving his business in the care of his brother.

After World War II and Marcello's death, his son Gino returned to New York and the pasta shop, which was then being run by a cousin. However, as the Italian population of the neighborhood dispersed, the business fell into a decline until non-Italian New Yorkers discovered Italian food. The business boomed after an article in a leading magazine declared Raffetto's pasta to be the best in the city.

Gino's sons now manage the business, and their mother, Romana, prepares the ten different pasta sauces herself. The shop not only provides its customers with ravioli stuffed with truffles, goat cheese, or arugula and ricotta among many other fillings, but also sells wholesale to some of New York's best Italian restaurants. Fettuccine, tagliatelle, pappardelle, and other noodle shapes are still cut on a machine that Marcello bought before 1917; the piece of equipment that rolls out the pasta dough only recently cracked and reluctantly had to be retired.

SAHADI IMPORTING COMPANY

187-189 ATLANTIC AVENUE (COURT-CLINTON
STREETS), BROOKLYN HEIGHTS
☎ (718) 624-4550
🚇 BOROUGH HALL (1/2/4/5)
MON-FRI: 9AM-7PM; SAT: 8:30AM-7PM
✦

ONCE THE FOOT OF WASHINGTON STREET
FROM BATTERY PLACE TO RECTOR STREET
was crowded with men in fezzes smoking hookahs,
with stores displaying the exotic wares of the
Levantine—colorful silks, beaded lampshades,
inlaid mother-of-pearl tables, hammered-brass pots,
and fragrant spices—and with coffeehouses, con-
fectionery shops, and restaurants offering unfamiliar
fare like shish kebab and baklava. The Arabs, Turks,
Armenians, and Greeks who settled here along the
western tip of Manhattan in the 1880s and '90s had
traveled only a few short blocks from the immigration stations at Castle Clinton and Ellis Island.

Among the Middle Eastern emporiums were
the store and manufacturing facility of Abraham
Sahadi from Zahle, Lebanon, who opened on
Washington Street in 1895, preparing and selling
bulgur wheat, tahini, halvah, toasted sesame seeds,
and more. Although the Sahadi wholesale business

was able to remain in the area until the 1960s, the Syrian Quarter was largely swept away by construction of the Brooklyn-Battery Tunnel in the late 1940s. Following most of the customers to the new Arab colony on Atlantic Avenue in Brooklyn was Abraham's nephew, Wade, whose retail branch of the business opened there in 1948.

The large Sahadi store has long been the anchor of the Little Lebanon commercial district, drawing shoppers of all ethnic backgrounds for the quality, selection, and prices of its merchandise. Imported grains, spices, beans, nuts, dried fruits, preserves, coffees, cheeses, breads, and two dozen kinds of olives are available. Prepared foods include hummus, baba ghanouj, couscous, tabbouleh, tatziki, hearts of palm, turnip pickles, stuffed grape leaves, lima bean salad, kibbeh (spiced ground lamb with pine nuts), and assorted rosewater-and-honey-drenched sweets.

IN BRIEF

RUSSO, 344 EAST 11TH STREET. Maker of stuffed pastas since 1908. The tiny shop also sells sauces, olives, cheese, sausages, and other Italian delicacies.

See also: MANGANARO'S (P. 175).

RESTAURANTS

✦

BRIDGE CAFÉ

279 WATER STREET (DOVER STREET)

☎ (212) 227-3344

🚇 BROOKLYN BRIDGE/CITY HALL (4/5/6)

DAILY: 11:45AM-MIDNIGHT

✦

IN THE ROUGH-AND-TUMBLE REALITY THAT WAS THE EARLY NEW YORK RIVERFRONT docks, the streets surrounding what is now the cleaned-up South Street Seaport were lined with bawdy taverns, gaming houses, and brothels, which in some buildings were conducting business on every floor. The 1855 census lists the prostitutes who worked in the premises that now house the Bridge Café; and an 1897 reform tract describes the building's saloon as "filled with river pirates and Water Street Hags."

The bar's checkered history as a drinking establishment—touted today as the oldest continuously run such enterprise in the city—dates back to 1794, when the structure contained a "grocer and wine and porter bottler." Throughout the years—straight through Prohibition and beyond—one saloon keeper after another operated here, a mere two blocks from City Hall.

The vintage interior has been maintained in the current bar and restaurant, although this is probably the first time that the old bead-board walls have ever been painted pale yellow and the pressed-tin ceiling lilac. Framed posters and photographs of the Brooklyn Bridge, which went up across the street in 1883; mounted chalkboards that list the daily specials; and a bare plank floor complete the simple décor. The Bridge Café is a great example of an old space that is comfortably inhabited by a modern-day establishment, with discerning business-types and locals from the downtown neighborhood the primary clientele. Overflow guests wait at the carved oak bar for one of the 20 or so tables to open up.

The Café's menu includes pumpkin ravioli with citrus butter and toasted almonds, grilled gulf shrimp over arugula with mango barbecue sauce, mussels in white wine with tarragon, chili-rubbed steak, rigatoni with sweet Italian sausage and shitake mushrooms in light garlic cream sauce, and buffalo steak with portobello mashed potatoes; for dessert, Key lime pie, espresso cheesecake, and white-chocolate gelato are among several offerings.

The Bridge Café is also available for private parties and weddings.

BROOKS 1890 RESTAURANT

24-28 JACKSON AVENUE (THOMSON AVENUE)
LONG ISLAND CITY, QUEENS
☎ (718) 937-1890   🚇 23RD ST/ELY AVE (E/V)
MON-FRI: 11AM-9PM

✦

ALTHOUGH SPARSELY POPULATED, LONG ISLAND CITY WAS A SEPARATE MUNICIpality in 1890 when a small bar opened on Jackson Avenue in a tidy brick building owned by the Bricklayers Union. Apart from the fact that the bar incorporated an upstairs social club called The Acorn, little is known about its founding story or, indeed, of its first 50 or so years in business. The architectural highlight, the distinctive stained-glass-embellished backbar, contains the interlocking initials "K" and "N" of the now-forgotten Jewish and Irish partners who owned and operated the place during Prohibition.

The current proprietors have maintained the name of Bill Brooks, who bought the restaurant in 1960, and they have preserved a large part of the original gaslight-era décor. The lunch crowd fills up the front barroom and back dining area for soups, sandwiches, burgers, salad platters, fresh fish, steaks, and Italian specialties.

FRAUNCES TAVERN

54 PEARL STREET (BROAD STREET)
☎ (212) 968-1776 🚇 WHITEHALL ST (N/R)
MON-FRI: 11:30AM-3PM; 5:30PM-9:30PM
SAT: 5:30PM-9:30PM

✦

THE HISTORY OF THE FLEDGLING UNITED STATES MIGHT BE COMPLETELY DIFFERENT had it not been for the actions of young Phoebe Fraunces. The serving girl at George Washington's headquarters at Richmond Hill is credited with foiling an attempt to assassinate the general with a dish of poisoned peas. Phoebe had been well taught by her father, Samuel, an ardent patriot, who was the proprietor of the Queen Charlotte Inn — named for the bride of King George III — at the corner of Pearl and Broad Streets. Even during the British occupation of New York, Fraunces, though kept a virtual prisoner on the premises, managed to work on behalf of the colonists, secretly aiding American prisoners of war. In the final days of the struggle, the newly christened Fraunces Tavern served for ten days as the general's last residence — meaning that Washington did indeed sleep here. And it was in the Tavern's Long Room that he famously delivered the tearful farewell to the officers of the Continental

Army on December 4, 1783, before returning to Mount Vernon.

The tavern, which steadily deteriorated during the nineteenth century and suffered damage in several fires, was finally rescued in 1904 from certain ruin by a patriotic organization dedicated to the preservation of Early American shrines. With only a scant description of the original premises, the tavern was reconstructed to look as it might have during Washington's day. It reopened with a colonial-style dining room at street level and a museum—featuring a re-creation of the paneled Long Room, complete with trestled tables, pewter tankards, and other period artifacts—on the upper floors. Decades later it was still so potent a symbol of America that, in 1975, the tavern was the target of a terrorist bomb attack by a Puerto Rican nationalist group, killing four.

Following a renovation in the late 1990s, visitors to the restaurant can once again dine on starters such as crab and shrimp cakes, tuna tartare, smoked salmon carpaccio, spicy Manhattan chowder, and main dishes such as wild striped bass with roasted beets, free-range chicken with a tomato-orange relish, pork tenderloin with grilled ratatouille, strip steak, meat loaf, pot roast, lobster roll, and burgers.

ONIEAL'S GRAND STREET BAR

174 GRAND STREET

(MULBERRY-CENTRE STREETS)

☎ (212) 941-9119   🚇 SPRING ST (6)

DAILY: 11:30AM-3PM, 5:30PM-11PM

✦

JOHN DILLINGER, AL CAPONE, AND ALL THE INFAMOUS GANGSTERS OF OLD NEW YORK passed through the ornate French Renaissance-style Police Headquarters at Grand and Centre Streets. After being booked, fingerprinted, interrogated, and having their mug shots taken, many detainees would be placed in a lineup. During the 1940s the photographer Weegee, chronicler of the vast New York underbelly, captured a particularly motley group being paraded from a paddy wagon into the building through a side entrance on Centre Market Place. This small cobblestone street was lined with gun dealers — John Jovins Distributor of Firearms and Police Equipment, established in 1911, still occupies an ancient brick building here — and was home to a saloon that was the watering hole of cops and newsmen on the crime beat. Teddy Roosevelt, the police commissioner before he was governor and president, often stepped across the street for a belt.

The bar — called Callahan's at some early point, then the Headquarters, then the Dutchman — had been open for some 30 years when the Police Building went up in 1909. A tunnel that still connects the two structures made possible discreet visits by cops to the upstairs brothel and to the bar itself during Prohibition. The most striking feature of the saloon was — and is — its remarkable Viennese-imported ceiling, a mahogany tour-de-force of hand-carved devils' heads, which just may have made the fallen souls who gathered beneath it feel more at home.

The Police Building was retired in 1973, leaving the bar without its traditional clientele. In 1996, the place was bought by the current owners, who reconceived the hard-drinking workingman's joint as an upscale bar, lounge, and restaurant. Now more wine than whiskey is drunk here (although there are quite a few single-malts available), and the menu runs to items such as hangar steak au poivre, roast chicken breast, bourbon-soaked barbequed short ribs, burgers, crab cakes, and frittatas.

THE PLAZA

768 FIFTH AVENUE (CENTRAL PARK SOUTH)

🚊 5TH AVE/59TH ST (N/R/W)

☎ OAK ROOM: (212) 546-5330

TUE-SAT: 5:30PM-10:30PM

☎ PALM COURT: (212) 546-5350

BREAKFAST: 6:30AM-11:30AM

LUNCH: NOON-2:30PM; TEA: 3:45PM-6PM

SUN BRUNCH: 10AM-2:30PM

✦

WHEN HENRY HARDENBERGH'S MASSIVE CHATEAU-LIKE APARTMENT BUILDING rose on Central Park West in 1884, it was so far from the center of town that people quipped it might as well be in Dakota—a name that stuck. At the time, shantytowns dotted the streets that surrounded the great park, which was still not entirely finished. Just 23 years later, the city had grown so much that no one considered Hardenbergh's majestic Plaza Hotel on Central Park South anything but the center of the universe. The French Renaissance-style edifice was immediately popular with elite visitors as well as well-heeled natives, who made the hotel's grand public rooms among the most fashionable in New York.

The Oak Room—named for the hand-carved paneling imported from England—was said to be

Hardenbergh's personal favorite in the hotel and is today one of the best-preserved. With murals that depict Bavarian castles, faux wine casks carved into the woodwork, and a brass chandelier adorned with bunches of grapes and a beer maiden hoisting a stein, this was a bastion of Edwardian male exclusivity. Celebrated men from the worlds of business and the arts, such as "Diamond" Jim Brady, Arturo Toscanini, Enrico Caruso, and George M. Cohan, who supposedly wrote some of his best-loved tunes here, were among the regulars. During the 1920s, F. Scott Fitzgerald and Ernest Hemingway were among the notable literary figures who spent time at the Oak Room. In its 62nd year, women were finally welcomed following a protest led by Betty Friedan and the National Organization for Women. The limited chophouse menu includes standards such as filet mignon, broiled salmon, prime rib, and veal chop.

If the Oak Room still feels like a male preserve, the light and airy Palm Court, also located on the main floor, was always intended for the ladies. Sometimes a harpist plays for the guests at high tea.

THE TONIC

108-110 WEST 18TH STREET
(SIXTH-SEVENTH AVENUES)
☎ (212) 929-9755
🚇 18TH ST (1/2); 14TH ST (F/V)
MON-SAT: NOON-3PM, 5:30PM-10:30PM

✦

LEGEND HAS IT THAT IN THE EARLY 1900S SILENT-FILM STARS USED TO GATHER after work in the saloon on West 18th Street that is now known as The Tonic. It may be true: the first film studio in the nation, American Mutoscope & Biograph Co., was founded in the mid-1890s on 14th Street between Sixth and Seventh Avenues, just four blocks south of the bar.

While it's tempting to imagine Biograph personalities D. W. Griffith, Mary Pickford, Mack Sennett, and the Gish sisters—Lillian and Dorothy —holding court at the beautiful long bar, the record, unfortunately, is sparse. The building was constructed in 1889 to house a saloon. As was often the case, a brewery—here Anheuser-Busch— contributed the bar, a mahogany masterpiece. The magnificent backbar, mirrors, and clock also date to 1889. The original owners are unknown, as is the name of their establishment. For a long time, a restaurant and bar called Harvey's Chelsea occupied the space. In 1992 the current proprietors opened a restaurant named 1889, which they replaced six years later with The Tonic.

In addition to a careful restoration of the mahogany treasures and an exact re-creation of the original tile floor, they've added lovely nineteenth-century Gothic-revival light fixtures that were salvaged from a church in Philadelphia, unusual vintage sconces and chandeliers from a Masonic Temple in Baltimore, and a climate-controlled glass-fronted wine cabinet that perfectly matches the backbar.

Both the dining room and the bar are pretty, spacious, and comfortable. The food is New American eclectic. Lunch features a pulled pork sandwich, torchon of foie gras with red-wine-poached quince, pomegranate-glazed salmon, and a sirloin burger. The dinner menu includes lobster carpaccio with fennel and baby arugula, basil-marinated grouper, barbecued pork chops, and muscat-glazed breast of duck. Saturday brunch choices include poached eggs with smoked salmon, white asparagus and herb butter; goat cheese galette with candied pecans, golden beets, and green apple; Maine crab crêpe with curried apple vinaigrette and cauliflower; and hanger steak au poivre. Desserts include a warm banana tart Tatin; the frozen lemon soufflé; the chocolate peanut butter tart; the cheese course; and espresso, cappuccino, four different press-pot coffees, and ten black, green, and herbal teas. The comprehensive international wine list comprises about 300 labels, 30 half-bottles, and 15 wines by the glass.

IN BRIEF

NIEDERSTEIN'S, 69-16 METROPOLITAN AVENUE, MIDDLE VILLAGE, QUEENS. Bavarian fare since 1889 in a onetime German neighborhood. The restaurant's large banquet room handles many private functions

SALOONS
& WINE SHOPS

continued

✦

ACKER, MERRALL & CONDIT

160 WEST 72ND STREET
(AMSTERDAM-COLUMBUS AVENUES)
☎ (212) 787-1700   🚇 72ND ST (1/2/3)
MON-SAT: 9AM-10PM

✦

WHEN ITS CONSIGNMENT OF 50 CASES OF WINE, 75 CASES OF ANCHOVIES, AND TEN cases of syrup went down with the Titanic in 1912, the grocers Acker, Merrall & Condit had already been in business for close to a century. At the time, the shop was located at the intersection of 72nd Street and Broadway, where it had landed after a number of uptown moves from its original 1820 location on Chambers Street.

Like most groceries of the period, Acker Merrall sold wine and spirits in addition to comestibles. Unlike those that favored the beverage side of the trade and evolved into saloons—the Bridge Café (p. 221), Fanelli's (p. 250)—Acker maintained its original mix. It was quite successful: by the turn of the twentieth century it had branches up and down the East Coast.

Ironically, although alcohol was not its mainstay, Prohibition, and perhaps the irrational exuberance of the Roaring '20s, deeply wounded Acker Merrall, and by the decade's end the company was bankrupt. Shortly after Repeal, however, a partnership revived the business, which the law now prohibited from selling groceries alongside wine and spirits. The new proprietors opted for the liquor license.

Today, Acker, Merrall & Condit — located since 1986 in a brownstone on 72nd Street — is among the city's finest wine shops. Long and narrow, with a barrel-vaulted ceiling and a slate-tile floor, it has the feeling of a cozy, well-lighted, and exceptionally well-stocked wine cellar.

In addition to a first-rate selection of wines, good prices, and a knowledgeable staff, Acker stocks Riedel glassware, bar accessories, and a selection of wine-related books and periodicals. The shop provides consulting services to clients looking to build or stock their cellars; it also organizes wine-intensive dinners, private wine tastings, and other special events. A sister company called The Wine Workshop conducts an impressive schedule of seminars. For restaurants, wine merchants, and serious collectors, Acker, which claims to be the largest independent auction house in the world, holds frequent auctions of rare and fine wines in New York and California. And for those who reside in cellarless dwellings, Acker provides climate-controlled, high-security storage lockers for rent.

THE ALGONQUIN

59 WEST 44TH STREET (FIFTH-SIXTH AVENUES)
☎ (212) 840-6800   🚇 42ND ST (B/D/F/V)
OAK ROOM—TUE-SAT: DINNER 7PM, SHOW 9PM
ROUND TABLE ROOM—BREAKFAST 7AM-10:30AM
LUNCH NOON-2:30PM; DINNER 5PM-10:30PM

✦

THE BARS AND RESTAURANTS OF THE ALGONQUIN HAD ALREADY BEEN SERVING cosmopolitan hotel visitors and New Yorkers for a generation before the legendary wits of the Round Table established the place as a literary landmark. Opened in 1902, just as the theater district was settling into the area, the hotel always drew a show business crowd—actors, agents, producers, playwrights—as well as writers from the offices of *Vanity Fair* magazine a few doors away. Starting in 1919, Robert Benchley, Robert Sherwood, Dorothy Parker, Alexander Wolcott, and Harpo Marx, among others, began to lunch at the hotel daily. Because they were little known beyond their own circle, the manager relegated them to the B-section Pergola Room (today's Oak Room). The long side table at which they gathered prompted the group to dub itself The Board, and then the Luigi Board, after the occult game that was currently the rage. Once the assembled began to rival the stature of those on the A-list (Florenz Ziegfield, the Barrymores, the Fairbankses, and their friends), they were relocated to the more prominent Rose Room (now the Round Table Room) right off the lobby and provided with a large round table, provoking a new name—The Vicious Circle.

A loving and respectful renovation in the late 1990s has restored the look and feel of both these rooms from decades ago. In the clubby Oak Room— with its eponymous paneling, its piano, and its leather chairs—dinner and cabaret performances are offered several nights a week. The Round Table Room, with volumes displayed in illuminated book-cases to reflect the room's great literary tradition, serves three meals a day and is a popular spot for breakfast meetings. Coffee, light snacks, and drinks are always available at the low upholstered settees in the potted-palm-filled lobby.

BILLY'S

948 FIRST AVENUE (52ND-53RD STREETS)
☎ (212) 355-8920   🚇 51ST ST (6)
DAILY: NOON-11PM

✦

"**I** ONLY REGRET THAT I HAVE BUT ONE LIFE TO GIVE FOR MY COUNTRY," PROCLAIMED 20-year-old Nathan Hale before he was hanged as a spy by the British, in September 1776, near First Avenue and 55th Street. At that time, of course, there was neither a First Avenue nor a 55th Street; the Upper East Side was still mainly field and forest, with the occasional farmhouse or inn.

Even by 1870 civilized Manhattan still extended no farther than 56th Street on the East Side. It was here that Mickey and Bridget Condron, recent arrivals from County Cork, Ireland, opened a tavern. The Condrons stuck to the basics: beer, sawdust on the floor, free food for those who continued to drink. Mickey's place—it had no other name—knew its clientele: local coal yard, tannery, slaughterhouse, and brewery workers. Mickey soon determined that a saloon ought to be on a corner, and in 1880 convinced the butcher at 55th Street to swap shops with him. It is not recorded if the trade worked for the butcher, but it succeeded brilliantly for Mickey. By the turn of the century his bar had become the place to see and be seen on the Upper East Side.

Mickey's son, Billy, joined the business in 1902, and around the time of World War I William Jr. came aboard as well. Both ignored Prohibition, and when new laws enacted after Repeal required bars to register under a formal name the place was formally christened Billy's.

In 1967 Billy's, now a full-fledged restaurant, was forced to relocate when its building was leveled to make way for a high-rise. A storefront was found just four blocks to the south, and all the fixtures and fittings — the carved-mahogany bar, the bellows-operated beer taps, the gas lamps, and the walk-in icebox — were moved. The outside may have changed, but the interior was instantly familiar to regulars.

Fourth-generation owner Joan Condron Borkowski now manages the business. The menu includes a lengthy list of high-end comfort foods: meat and potatoes, a chopped-shrimp or grilled-cheese-and-bacon sandwich, a hamburger with a side of onion rings, rice pudding. Fresh seasonal fish is always available; lovers of soft-shell crabs consider Billy's to be among the city's best. A Berenice Abbott photo of the two Billys hangs above the bar where they served their customers for so many years.

BOHEMIAN HALL

29-19 24TH AVENUE

(29TH-31ST STREETS) ASTORIA, QUEENS

☎ (718) 728-9776   🚇 ASTORIA BLVD (N/W)

FRI: 5PM-4AM; SAT-SUN: NOON-4AM

ADDITIONAL SUMMER HOURS:

WED-THUR 5PM-4AM

✦

IN THE WANING DAYS OF THE NINETEENTH CENTURY, HARRY HOUDINI WAS ONE OF MANY colorful performers who entertained crowds at scores of the city's boisterous beer halls. These multifaceted establishments, which often incorporated bars, dining rooms, and ballrooms, were mostly run by and for German immigrants. In the summer, sprawling outdoor beer gardens provided a welcome respite for dwellers of stifling tenement apartments. While a few beer halls managed to stay in business into the 1950s, today only one remains in all of New York City, a Czech, not German, establishment located in Astoria, Queens.

The large Czech colony that had fled Austro-Hungarian repression and made its way to Queens formed, in 1892, the Bohemian Citizens' Benevolent Society, wistfully named after the vanished Middle European kingdom. The Society purchased a patch of farmland in Astoria, and members raised money—at a penny a brick—until they were able to build a community center called Bohemian Hall. The first section was completed in 1910; the last section—an expansive outdoor beer garden—in 1919, just before Prohibition temporarily sent beer drinkers indoors and underground.

Today, from Memorial Day through Oktoberfest, visitors seated at old-fashioned wooden picnic tables can drink a good Czech pilsner and eat a hamburger or kielbasa cooked on charcoal grills at the Bohemian Hall beer garden. The indoor bar and downstairs restaurant are open year-round and could easily be mistaken for a VFW outpost anywhere in America—except for the many Czech signs and framed pictures of Czech national heroes. The frequently updated menu, in English and Czech, may include headcheese with vinegar, onion and bread; goulash soup; roast duck with potato dumplings and sweet red cabbage; roast pork with pear butter and french fries; and chicken paprikash with dumplings.

CHUMLEY'S

86 BEDFORD STREET (BARROW-GROVE STREETS)
☎ (212) 675-4449
🚇 CHRISTOPHER ST/SHERIDAN SQ (1/2)
MON-FRI: 5PM-MIDNIGHT; SAT-SUN: 11AM-2AM
CASH ONLY

✦

IN THE 1830S, WHAT IS NOW CHUMLEY'S DINING ROOM WAS A BLACKSMITH'S SHOP with a stable out back. Connecting the two was an open area where coaches entering through Pamela Court stopped and allowed passengers to disembark. Both the laneway and the blacksmith's shop were unmarked and difficult to find — perhaps deliberately. According to legend, this was a stop on the Underground Railroad, complete with a secret tunnel out to Grove Street. From there it was a short passage to the black community of Gay Street, where runaway slaves could start life anew.

By the turn of the century the blacksmith's shop had become a garage, and the Underground Railroad stop had become a secret meeting place and canteen for people with underground opinions — people like the Wobblies, the radical Industrial Workers of the World. Police raids were not uncommon. In about 1922, Leland Chumley, a

Wobbly organizer who had at one time been a stage-coach driver, a railroad laborer, a soldier of fortune, and a waiter, took over and began renovating the place as a restaurant, speakeasy, and gambling den.

Chumley opened the still-unmarked doors to the public, and although the police raids continued, it was under the friendlier, more corrupt terms that were common during the period: the cops would phone ahead, warning, "We're coming through the 86 Bedford entrance — tell your customers." This was shortened to "86 the customers," and ultimately to the now-ubiquitous "86."

With its rich history and colorful owner, the saloon was a hit with the literary crowd, even after Repeal. The roster of renowned customers — John Dos Passos, Edna St. Vincent Millay, John Reed, Theodore Dreiser, Ring Lardner, Allen Ginsberg, Sinclair Lewis, John Steinbeck, James Thurber, Willa Cather, Ernest Hemingway, Jack Kerouac, Lillian Hellman, Eugene O'Neill, Anaïs Nin, E. E. Cummings, William Burroughs, Norman Mailer, Simone de Beauvoir, F. Scott Fitzgerald — is almost endless. When a regular's book was published, Lee Chumley hung the cover on the wall. His wife, Henrietta, who took over when he died in 1935, sustained the tradition, as did Ray Santini, the former bartender who bought it in 1960, as do Steve

Shlopak and Bill Butler, who have owned the place since 1987.

Despite its rough-and-tumble tradition, the Chumley's of today is warm and cozy, especially in the winter when logs are crackling in the fireplace. The menu includes spicy chicken wings, fried calamari, and fish and chips; salmon, roast duck, and rib-eye steak; burgers and shepherd's pies; several salads; and a good pasta selection.

A recent tradition, dating back to the Watt Street fire of 1994, is that all Chumley's bartenders are off-duty firefighters from nearby Engine 24-Ladder 5. When asked, they're happy to point out the trapdoor over the old Underground Railroad tunnel.

P. J. CLARKE'S

915 THIRD AVENUE (55TH STREET)

☎ (212) 759-1650

🚇 LEXINGTON AVE/53RD ST (E/V)

✦

BEFORE THE DAYS OF BOTTLING PLANTS
AND CORNER GROCERS, NEW YORKERS
either consumed beer in a saloon or lugged it home
in a bucket. In order to expedite the takeout process,
and keep bucketed beer from sloshing on people at
the bar, some taverns installed a special window.
The customer passed in an empty pail, got it back
brimming with sudsy brew, and paid—all without
entering the premises. Perhaps the last remaining
beer window in town is the one through the wall of
P. J. Clarke's, a bar that has preserved almost all of
its old-time saloon trappings. There's the men's
room, a shed enclosing colossal vintage urinals
under a stained-glass dome, the carved mahogany
woodwork, ancient streaked mirrors, worn tile floor,
tin ceiling, and portraits of Lincoln, FDR, and JFK
hung above the bar.

The Third Avenue El rumbled overhead when
Ehret's brewery built the tavern in 1890, one of
many Irish bars in the resolutely working-class
neighborhood. Patrick Joseph Clarke took over the

place in 1904 and ran it until he died after World War II. His heirs sold out to the building's owner, an antiques dealer named Daniel H. Lavezzo Jr., whose benign neglect maintained the bar's patina for another half century. It was said that on any given night the patrons might include Marilyn Monroe, Hubert Humphrey, and mobster Frank Costello. Lavezzo, who refused to sell the building when developers wanted to tear it down for a high-rise, negotiated a deal that traded the little brick building's air rights for a long lease and more than a million dollars.

Although for years the executives who toiled in the nearby towers packed it to capacity, P. J. Clarke's declared bankruptcy in 2002. Lavezzo's son, Daniel H. III, sold to a restaurant group who have insisted that they won't do away with any of the eccentricities that make the place: the notepads on which customers jot down their own orders, the quirky pricing scheme — $12.40, $18.10, $4.90 — the broken phone booth, or the moth-eaten stuffed dog that sits on a bar shelf.

Menu highlights include Caesar salad, smoked trout over arugula, grilled shrimp with bacon, corned beef and cabbage, chicken pot pie, eggs Benedict, and burgers.

EAR INN

326 SPRING STREET

(GREENWICH-WASHINGTON STREETS)

☎ (212) 226-9060   🚇 SPRING ST (C/E)

DAILY: NOON-4AM

✦

O N NEW YEAR'S DAY, 1800, THE MURDER OF A YOUNG QUAKER MAIDEN, GUILIELMA Sands, alarmed the local populace. The body was discovered in a well fed by the spring after which Spring Street, the lane that ran past it, was named. The young man who had been courting her was charged with the murder and then cleared by his gifted attorneys, Alexander Hamilton and Aaron Burr, just four years before the duel that has linked their names together forever. The crime scene attracted hundreds of curiosity seekers, and local papers reported repeated sightings of Guilielma's mournful ghost.

Throughout the years, other ghosts have been seen and heard at another Spring Street location, the Ear Inn, a wonderfully eccentric tavern housed in a two-story Federal townhouse constructed in 1817 at the Hudson River end of the street. The builder was a successful tobacco trader named James Brown, who may or may not have been an aide to George

Washington and who may or may not be the black man pictured in Cass Gilbert's famous painting of the general crossing the Delaware. By the middle of the nineteenth century, the house was a brewery, serving corn whisky to the sailors and longshoremen toiling along the bustling piers; the rooms upstairs were used as a boarding house, a smugglers' den, a bordello, and eventually as a speakeasy during Prohibition. For years, the premises was nameless; then, in the 1970s, the owners daubed a bit of black paint on the neon sign, changing "Bar" to "Ear," gaining a name while avoiding having to seek city approval of a new sign.

Live music and poetry readings have replaced sea chanties and pool games, but little else has changed here. The bar in the front room is decorated with old crocks, bottles, and jugs that were unearthed during the construction of the back dining room that was added at the turn of the century. There is not a straight line or right angle in either of these rooms, where customers relax with a drink and a burger, omelet, salad, or sandwich. The vintage maritime décor — model boats, mounted fish, porthole covers, a life preserver, etchings of the New York waterfront — and the old boat cleats out front are reminders that this building once sat just five feet from the banks of the Hudson.

FANELLI'S CAFÉ

94 PRINCE STREET (MERCER STREET)
☎ (212) 226-9412 🚇 PRINCE ST (R)
MON-THUR: 10AM-2:30AM
FRI-SAT: 10AM-3:30AM; SUN: 11AM-2:30AM

✦

JUST TEN YEARS INTO THE NEW NINE-
TEENTH CENTURY, NEW YORK'S CITY HALL
building was nearing completion at the northern-
most edge of town, on lower Broadway. The southern, eastern, and western sides of the elegant
French Renaissance-style edifice were sheathed in
gleaming white marble. The back — north — side of
what Henry James called a "divine little structure,"
however, was faced with simple brownstone: as the
city was not expected to expand past this point, no
one was meant to see it. In spite of these modest
expectations for the city's growth, Broadway was
soon paved to Astor Place, a mile north of here.

By the Civil War, luxury hotels and fashionable
emporia — Tiffany (p. 189), Brooks Brothers (p. 66),
Lord & Taylor (p. 69) — did a brisk business along the
stretch of the thoroughfare that passed through
what a century and a half later would come to be
known as SoHo. If Broadway was the great stage
upon which all the dramas of the city's elite society

were played out, then backstreets like Mercer, running parallel just one block away, became the ultimate backstage — lined with opulent bordellos and other businesses that depended on the carriage trade along Broadway but couldn't show their faces there.

A five-story brick building at the corner of Mercer and Prince Street was typical, with a porterhouse in its storefront and an expensive brothel upstairs. It had replaced a more modest wooden structure that housed a grocer and spirits dealer as far back as 1847 — a geneology that allows Fanelli's Café on the site today to call itself "the second oldest continuous food and drink establishment on the same site in New York." After the war, as the better shops and hotels kept pace with the city's onward march up Broadway, the area eventually became a gritty warehouse and factory district. The saloon at 94 Prince — run from 1878 to 1902 by the Nicholas Gerdes whose name is etched in the glass transom above the entrance — became a classic workingman's bar until the next major change to the neighborhood, in the 1960s, brought a whole new clientele into the mix. At first viewed with suspicion, the painters and sculptors who found studio space in the cast-iron loft buildings eventually won over the proprietor, Michael Fanelli, the former boxer and benign curmudgeon who made the bar what it is today.

Calling his place a café was a smart move in 1922, at the start of Prohibition, when Fanelli began his 60-year tenure as owner. The speakeasy made wine and distilled bathtub gin in the cellar, and purchased hard booze from bootleggers, keeping the stash in a secret room — which can still be reached through one of the lower cupboards in the elaborately carved backbar — hidden under the stairs. Fanelli kept the place much as it had been since the beautiful fixtures and the fleur-de-lis tile floor were installed. He did hang photos of fighters he admired, and some whom he promoted, and posted the sign that designated the back section the "Ladies & Gents sitting room," today the quieter, no-smoking section of the bar.

The current owners, the Noe family, have also resisted making any "improvements" to this classic New York interior, a restraint appreciated by the loyal group of regulars, SoHo shoppers, and tourists. And all enjoy Fanelli's better-than-typical pub-food menu: omelets, quiches, pizza, soups, sandwiches, burgers, chili (meat and vegetarian), steak frites, shepherd's pie, blackened catfish, fish and chips, pan-seared salmon, mussels, lasagna, linguini with pesto, and salads.

P. J. HANLEY'S TAVERN

449 COURT STREET (NELSON STREET)
CARROLL GARDENS, BROOKLYN
☎ (718) 834-8223   🚇 CARROLL ST (F/G)
MON-WED: 5PM-11PM; THUR-SUN: NOON-11PM
CASH ONLY

✦

A CENTURY BEFORE THE FILM ON THE WATERFRONT, THE PIERS AND SHIPYARDS of Red Hook were alive with the native tongues of sailors from around the world and of immigrant dockworkers — Irish, Italians, Arabs, and Norwegians. The largest community of Norwegians in New York grew up in the surrounding streets, with organizations like the Norwegian Seamen's Church, and establishments like the Norwegian-owned saloon that opened in 1874 at the corner of Court and Nelson Streets, catering to them. Despite its Scandinavian origins, however, the place is now known as one of the handful of century-old Irish bars because in 1898, as more and more Irish workers flooded into the neighborhood, a Jack Ryan bought the property.

Ryan ran the saloon for nearly 60 years, simply blacking out the windows during Prohibition and brewing his own beer in tanks that only recently were removed from behind the bar. P. J. Hanley took over in 1956, selling to two nieces in the mid-1990s. How well these few owners have preserved the place is apparent in a sepia-toned photograph that hangs on the walls today. Except for the absence of stools, the long, elaborately carved bar looks the same, with bowler-hatted young gents standing beside the prodigious elbow rail. And although ladies could not be served there, a separate drinking room was set up for them behind a partition.

Shepherd's pie, chicken pot pie, burgers, buffalo wings, individual pan pizzas, and a daily soup, fish, and pasta are available in the adjoining dining rooms or on the large outdoor patio in good weather.

JULIUS

159 WEST TENTH STREET
(WAVERLY PLACE-SEVENTH AVENUE SOUTH)
☎ (212) 929-9672
📱 CHRISTOPHER ST/SHERIDAN SQ (1/2)
SUN-THUR: 11AM-2AM; FRI-SAT: 11AM-4AM

✦

IN 1833, ADMIRERS OF SIR WALTER SCOTT'S
NOVEL WAVERLEY SUCCESSFULLY PETITIONED
the city to have a street in Greenwich Village named
in the Englishman's honor. There had recently been
several notable structures erected on the street,
including the noble residences known as "The Row"
(along the stretch that bordered Washington Square
Park) and the Northern Dispensary (a public clinic at
the curious intersection where the street makes an
idiosyncratic branch of itself). A block west of here,
a three-story frame house was built with a dry-goods
establishment at its street level. Of these, the last is
the most changed.

The premises became a tavern in the years after
the Civil War and remained one through Prohibition,
when, with boarded-up windows, it was known as the
Seven Doors. After Repeal, it gained the name Julius,
though no one is sure whether it was in honor of the
owner's basset hound, one of the bartenders, or both.

Although the Village began to attract growing numbers of homosexuals by the 1920s, Julius did not become a gay hangout until the 1950s, and then only in the back room. At the time of the Stonewall Riot around the corner on Christopher Street, however, Julius allowed itself to be used by a gay rights organization in a test case to fight the law that prevented bars from serving declared homosexuals.

Today, Julius is the oldest gay bar in the city.

KENN'S BROOME STREET BAR

363 WEST BROADWAY (BROOME STREET)
☎ (212) 925-2086 🚇 SPRING ST (C/E)
DAILY: 11AM-2AM

✦

THE NEIGHBORHOOD OF SOHO HAS CHANGED AS MUCH AS ANY NEIGHBORHOOD IN NEW York City. Going back through time, its celebrated cast-iron loft buildings have housed an upscale shopping district, an artists' quarter, and a center of light industry and warehouses. But the area had a life, albeit a sedate one, long before then, when this part of Manhattan was well out in the country, far north of the little city at the tip of the island. Among the clusters of small Federal-style houses was the one at 63-65 Prince Street where the destitute former president James Monroe came to live with his daughter before dying on Independence Day, 1831.

Another nearby historic structure from the early nineteenth century is the small landmarked building that houses Kenn's Broome Street Bar, which was built sometime around 1825 and may be the oldest structure in SoHo. A bar and restaurant have operated here since the 1850s, with a variety of different names, owners, and clientele. One incarnation, a German beer hall from the 1880s, added the stained-glass panels above the windows. For many years, the bar was popular with truckers on their way to the nearby Holland Tunnel entrance. The current establishment dates from the period when painters and sculptors began moving to the neighborhood, finding studio space in the loft buildings with their high ceilings and large windows. A number of artists — Willem De Kooning, Claes Oldenburg, and, later, Keith Haring — hung out at Kenn's, posting ad hoc creations beside the menu listings on the black chalkboard-covered walls.

Today's menu includes burgers, the typical sandwiches (as well as less usual ones such as sardines with cream cheese, watercress, and red onion) and salads (Chinese with tofu, baby corn, cold noodles, and water chestnuts; Mediterranean with roasted peppers and feta cheese). The well-priced pub food suits the place, with its jukebox serenading those seated at the plain wooden bar stools or at tables in the larger back room.

LANDMARK TAVERN

626 11TH AVENUE (46TH STREET)
☎ (212) 757-8595
🚊 42ND ST/PORT AUTHORITY (A/C/E)
DAILY: NOON-MIDNIGHT

✦

SLAUGHTERHOUSES, STOCKYARDS, LUMBER-
YARDS, STABLES, GLUE FACTORIES, SHACKS
and shanties—this was the far West Side of mid-
Manhattan just after the Civil War. The streets were
crowded with unskilled immigrant laborers, with
sailors and longshoremen from the nearby docks,
and with the taverns, gambling dens, boarding
houses, and brothels that catered to them. In 1868,
before landfill pushed the shoreline westward past
12th Avenue, Patrick Henry Carley built an Irish
saloon at what was then the water's edge, 11th
Avenue. It has outlasted them all.

Where nickel beers were once pumped at the
distinctive mahogany bar—turned from a single
solid tree trunk—customers at the Landmark
Tavern now sample some of the 60 or so single-malt
scotches. Despite the changes, the front and rear
dining rooms are still warmed by wood-burning
potbellied stoves. Potato soup with hickory bacon,
Scotch eggs, fish and chips, crab cakes, country-style

pork chops, steaks, and shepherd's pie are among the classic menu offerings. Selections from the raw bar are shucked to order; at brunch, Irish soda bread is baked fresh every hour. Many of the recipes are Carley's originals.

Although it is no longer a dock bar serving hard-drinking seamen from around the globe, the customers remain international — New Yorkers as well as tourists visiting the area's theaters, the Javits Center, and the Intrepid, among other local attractions.

The upstairs rooms, where Mrs. Carley raised the children, and which became a speakeasy during Prohibition, are now available for private parties.

MARE CHIARO

176 ½ MULBERRY STREET
(GRAND-BROOME STREETS)
☎ (212) 226-9345
🚇 SPRING ST (6); GRAND ST (S)
MON-SAT: 10:30AM-5AM, SUN: NOON-5AM

✦

ALTHOUGH THE REGULARS—AND THE CROWD HERE IS MOSTLY REGULARS—PROBABLY know the name of the joint, they don't use it much. Around the neighborhood Mare Chiaro is called the Sinatra Bar. The formal name, which can be translated as "clear sea," is, in fact, highly unsuited to what must be one of the least clear spaces in the entire city. Smoking, preferably a cigar, is all but mandatory, and there is little evidence of a functioning ventilation system. The regulars don't mind; they're too busy smoking to notice.

Frank Sinatra first drank here in 1941. For an Italian-American celebrity looking to escape the clamoring hordes at swank Midtown nightclubs, it was the perfect retreat after a performance or a lovers' quarrel. There is a photograph in the window that commemorates the establishment's most famous former regular. It shows the owner, Tony Tenneriello, proudly holding another photo, taken in the bar, of himself, his wife, and Ol' Blue Eyes.

Mare Chiaro was founded, in what was once the heart of Little Italy, by Tenneriello's father in 1908, five years after he arrived from Naples. The pressed-tin ceiling, elaborate carved-wood bar, vintage room divider, tile floor, and much else are original. The cash register is old. The Formica-and-chrome kitchenette tables, though of a more recent vintage, are still old. The pictures on the wall are old. About the only concessions to the modern world are the jukebox, the videogame machine, and the TV, tuned to sports. In its early days the bar served food and drink. (During Prohibition, the food was accompanied by homemade wine.) In the mid-1970s, Tenneriello decided that food was superfluous, and the regulars of today know they must dine either before or after they visit the Sinatra Bar.

MC SORLEY'S OLD ALE HOUSE

15 EAST SEVENTH STREET

(SECOND-THIRD AVENUES)

☎ (212) 473-9148 🚇 ASTOR PL (6)

MON-SAT: 11AM-1AM; SUN: 1PM-1AM

✦

ON A SNOWY FEBRUARY NIGHT IN 1860 A FORMER CONGRESSMAN FROM ILLINOIS named Abraham Lincoln made his way to the Great Hall at Cooper Union, where he had been invited to deliver the speech that would propel him to national prominence and the presidency. The school of mechanical arts and sciences had been erected just one year earlier — Mark Twain had given the auditorium's inaugural address — by philanthropist Peter Cooper. One of Cooper's closest friends was a barkeep named John McSorley, who had opened a pub in 1854 just around the corner. Of the few surviving drinking establishments that were doing business during Lincoln's lifetime, McSorley's is the only one that can claim him as a customer.

Joseph Mitchell wrote brilliantly about this historic bar in *McSorley's Wonderful Saloon* back in 1942. McSorley's has barely changed since. Mitchell reports that the place "is equipped with electricity, but the bar is stubbornly illuminated with a pair of gas lamps, which flicker fitfully and throw shadows on the low, cobwebby ceiling each time someone opens the street door." He tells of the four soup bowls — for nickels, dimes, quarters, and half-dollars — that are used instead of a cash register, of the rickety chairs and potbellied stove, of the old black safe, of the crock of tobacco and rack of clay and corncob pipes. During Prohibition, we learn, there was no peephole, no protection paid, and no raids; a retired brewer from the Bronx produced ale in a row of washtubs in the cellar.

John McSorley never sampled the bathtub brew, having died at 87 in 1910. He passed the saloon to his son Bill, who was so sensitive to any alteration of his father's hallowed place that he wept inconsolably when essential repairs were made to the sagging bar. Twenty-five years later, Bill sold the saloon to a retired policeman on the condition that no changes be willingly made. When the cop died just four years later, his daughter inherited McSorley's but never entered during hours, respecting Old John's dictum that it is "impossible for men to drink with tranquility in the presence of women."

Women were finally — famously — allowed to drink at McSorley's in 1970, 116 years after its opening, only when it became illegal for the saloon to forbid them entry.

OLD TOWN

45 EAST 18TH STREET

(BROADWAY-PARK AVENUE SOUTH)

☎ (212) 529-6732

🚇 14TH ST/UNION SQ (4/5/6/L/N/Q/R/W)

DAILY: NOON-MIDNIGHT

✦

IN THE BOOM YEARS FOLLOWING THE CIVIL WAR, UNION SQUARE—NAMED NEITHER FOR the Union Army nor for the labor unions that have traditionally rallied here, but for the union of the Bowery and Broadway — was home to theaters, concert halls, and exclusive shops. Among these were a large number of German-owned businesses along 14th Street — FAO Schwarz (p. 91), Steinway Hall and the company's piano showroom (p. 325), the German Savings Bank, and a half-dozen German beer halls, including the famed Luchow's, which lasted exactly 100 years, from 1882 to 1982. Just north of the square, Viemeister's, a Teutonic-style saloon, supplied by one of the German breweries in Yorkville, opened in 1892. It is still very much in business.

The beautifully preserved turn-of-the-century interior features the requisite vintage tile floor, etched glass, stained glass, beveled mirrors, and a pressed-tin ceiling that makes a compelling case for the ills of smoking: last painted white on Election Day, 1952, it has been stained a deep, dark nicotine brown. The gas fixtures mounted outside the saloon were used by departing customers to hail passing trolleys. The high, leather-upholstered booths contain hidden bins where drinks could be stashed during Prohibition-era raids. After Repeal, another German family, the Lohdens, purchased Viemeister's and changed its name to the Old Town.

The bar and the coveted booths fill quickly at lunch, in the evenings, and on weekends, making the ancient dumbwaiter work overtime delivering burgers, salads, shepherd's pie, meat loaf, chili, and other hearty pub food from the kitchen upstairs, where additional, no-smoking tables are available.

THE PARIS BAR & GRILL

119 SOUTH STREET (PECK SLIP)
☎ (212) 240-9797   🚊 FULTON ST (1/2)
DAILY: NOON–4AM

✦

SITUATED RIGHT ON THE EAST RIVER
WATERFRONT, MEYER'S HOTEL WAS HANDY
to sailing ships that docked at the nearby piers, to
the Long Island-bound ferries, and to the powerful
commercial interests of lower Manhattan. Such
notables as Thomas Edison, "Buffalo Bill" Cody,
Annie Oakley, Butch Cassidy, and the Sundance Kid
are known to have stayed here. Furthermore, during
its first decade, the hotel, which opened in 1873,
provided its guests front-row seats on the construction of the colossal Brooklyn Bridge just outside its
windows. To further enhance his property, the enter-
prising Henry Meyer added a large, welcoming barroom, outfitted with all the most stylish accoutrements of the day and named for the most elegant
city in the world — the Paris Café.

Although the hotel is long gone, the refurbished
saloon is very much alive, drawing a Wall Street
crowd to its long, U-shaped oak bar. In the bilevel
back dining room, with a singularly beautiful pressed-
tin ceiling and vintage prints of the surrounding area

in olden days, diners order from a menu that includes steamed mussels, fried calamari, chicken wings, Caesar salad, sesame-crusted tuna, grilled salmon, several sandwiches, pastas, and burgers.

PETE'S TAVERN

129 EAST 18TH STREET (IRVING PLACE)

☎ (212) 473-7676

🚇 14TH ST/UNION SQ (4/5/6/L/N/Q/R/W)

DAILY: 11:30AM-MIDNIGHT

✦

DURING PROHIBITION, CUSTOMERS ENTERED
THE POPULAR SPEAKEASY AT 18TH STREET
and Irving Place through the refrigerated showcase
of a tiny florist shop that was built to conceal the
old-time Irish saloon that had been on that corner
for half a century.

The first occupant of the premises had been a
small grocery and spirits shop that opened in 1851,
when the lovely Gramercy Park, two blocks away,
was only two decades old. The park's visionary
developer, Samuel Ruggles, had named the street in
honor of his good friend Washington Irving. A
saloon called Healy's took over the property by 1864
and became a hangout for politicos from the Irish-
dominated Tammany Hall nearby on 14th Street.
Literary figures were also at home here, and it is
said that one of the regulars, William Henry
Porter — better known as O. Henry — actually
wrote "Gift of the Magi" at the first booth by the
door. After Repeal, Pete — Peter Belles — bought

the place from the gangster bootleggers who had been running it illegally. When Pete left in the mid 1950s, the saloon acquired the back room from a tailor shop and adopted an Italian menu.

The bar — with three TVs and a loud juke-box — remains very popular, filling up in the early evening with people stopping in on their way home from work for a draft beer drawn from the old porcelain taps. The restaurant is still Italian — garlic bread, fried zucchini, pastas, veal marsala, sausage and peppers — but also offers chicken wings, coconut shrimp, chicken Kiev, and burgers.

SCOTTO'S WINE CELLAR

318 COURT STREET (SACKETT-DEGRAW STREETS)
CARROLL GARDENS, BROOKLYN
☎ (718) 875-5530 🚇 CARROLL ST (F/G)
MON-SAT: 9AM-9PM

✦

ONE OF THE CONSEQUENCES OF AN ITAL-
IAN MOTHER'S DESIRE, IN 1910, TO SPEND
more time with her son is that there is a good wine
store today on Court Street.

Young Domenico Scotto, from the tiny island of
Procida north of Capri in the Bay of Naples, arrived
in Brooklyn in 1903 with two métiers: winemaking
and ship caulking. When he learned that most of
the latter work had recently moved from the
Brooklyn waterfront to shipyards several states to
the south, he reinvented himself as a caulking contractor, constantly traveling back and forth along the
Eastern Seaboard seeking work for other immigrants. He was making a good living — good enough
to bring his mother over from the old country. She
had just one complaint: she never got to see him.
And so he gave up the contracting business and,
with his brothers, opened a wine store on Hicks
Street in Red Hook. (Most of the street was swept
away in the 1950s by the construction of the

Brooklyn-Queens Expressway.) The Scottos provided clay jugs emblazoned with their name, which customers filled with wine from the barrels in the store. Some of the wine was imported from Europe, some came from California, and some was made by Italian winemakers down the street.

When Prohibition shuttered the store in 1919, the Scottos leapt into the booming movie-theater business, building one on Court Street and leasing others. They continued in the beverage business, delivering ferro kino, a quinine-based "tonic" containing a significant amount of alcohol, to local speakeasies until the authorities caught on. After Repeal, they secured one of the city's first new wine licenses and reopened at the current location.

Even after family friend James Benedetto took over the shop in 1989, one of Domenico's sons, Leo Scotto, continued to work there until he died, in his 80s, just before Christmas, 2001.

TEDDY'S BAR & GRILL

96 BERRY STREET (NORTH EIGHTH STREET)
NORTHSIDE, BROOKLYN
☎ (718) 384-9787   🚊 BEDFORD AVE (L)
SUN-THUR: 11AM-MIDNIGHT; FRI-SAT:11AM-2AM

+

THE PARENTS OF THE BEAUTIFUL BAVARIAN-BORN MATILDA DOELGER BOYCOTTED HER Brooklyn wedding, in 1889, to an unemployed boxer named John West. The Doelgers, successful owners of a brewery, eventually overcame their disapproval, and provided the young couple with an apartment above a tavern the brewery franchised in working-class Northside where the Wests raised three children, Mildred Katharina, John Edwin, and the apple of her mother's eye, Mary Jane.

Matilda, whose family had also thwarted her dream of becoming an actress, dressed her adorable blond daughter in fancy clothes, gave her dancing lessons, and had her performing in public by the age of five. Little Mary Jane West, known by her nickname, Mae, loved the spotlight so much that she stayed in it for the rest of her life.

There is no plaque commemorating Mae West on the four-story brick building, but the tavern does still bear her relation's name — "Peter Doelger's

Extra Beer"—emblazoned across its façade in stained glass. This fortunate piece of architectural preservation is all the more remarkable considering that, from 1920 on, no one was officially watching over this lovely sign: the brewery never reopened after Prohibition. The tavern itself has survived, in near-original condition, thanks to a succession of sympathetic owners.

In the late 1980s, Felice Kirby, Glenn Kirby, and Lee Ornati bought the former Doelger bar from Teddy and Mary Prusik. Teddy's today is a friendly saloon, a good restaurant, and a great place to hear music. A deejay spins disks three evenings a week; there's also occasional live music and a monthly tap-dance jam. When no one is performing, there's a terrific jukebox. The front room is a classic high-ceilinged bar, especially beautiful with sunlight streaming through that stained-glass sign. The back room is smaller and, in wintertime, with logs aflame in the fireplace, very cozy. Lunch and dinner menus are eclectic, with an array of international starters and entrees such as a duck wrap with mandarin orange horseradish, a "salmon BLT" with dill mayonnaise, pan-seared catfish, burgers, and a toasted Cubano sandwich. The brunch menu features crab cakes Benedict, a breakfast burrito, corned beef hash with eggs, and a gargantuan Bloody Mary.

WALKER'S

16 NORTH MOORE STREET (VARICK STREET)
☎ (212) 941-0142   🚇 FRANKLIN ST (1/2)
DAILY: NOON-1AM

✦

THE AREA IMMEDIATELY BELOW CANAL STREET WAS, IN THE LATE 1600S, FARM-land owned largely by Trinity Church. As the city expanded from the south, the parish developed the land, building solid red-brick townhouses to lure the wealthy. Within two generations the prosperous residents were fleeing farther uptown as commercial interests overran the district. By the late nineteenth century, when it was one of the busiest industrial neighborhoods in Manhattan, any remaining resi-dences were dwarfed by stately loft buildings with cast-iron façades.

In 1890, a savvy real estate developer, observing that local laborers had few places to go for a drink after work, built a high-ceilinged corner saloon with four stories of apartments above it. The neighbor-hood flourished for a few decades, as did the bar. Then, as the Depression hit and manufacturing jobs disappeared, they both began a slow descent. By the mid 1930s the building at North Moore and Varick had become a single-room-occupancy hotel above a shabby bar. In the '40s the storefront was an Irish restaurant, in the '50s a Spanish place, in the '60s a shot-and-beer joint. By the late 1980s, most of the factories below Canal Street were gone, their former buildings prime targets for conversion to living-lofts by the same kinds of people who had earlier resurrected SoHo.

The team that owned the Ear Inn (p. 248) bought the bar in 1987 and promptly went to work stripping paint from wood, acoustic tiles from ceilings, linoleum from floors, and 1950s-vintage wood paneling from walls. When the renovation was complete, the place looked much the way it had the day it opened in 1890 — with a thoroughly modern menu. In addition to the de rigueur burgers, there's hummus and pita with fresh lemon juice and an olive-oil drizzle; chili-dusted grilled shrimp with roasted tomatillo sauce; a tasty yellowfin tuna Niçoise wrap; potato-crusted salmon fillet; and chopped sirloin with green peppercorn demi-glace over mashed potatoes. The food is good, the service is friendly, and the mahogany bar, restored to its original grandeur, surely stocks a wider range of libations than in any of the establishment's previous incarnations.

WHITE HORSE TAVERN

567 HUDSON STREET (11TH STREET)
☎ (212) 243-9260
🚇 14TH ST (A/C/E); 8TH AVE (L)
DAILY: 11AM-2AM
CASH ONLY

✦

WHEN DYLAN THOMAS FAMOUSLY DRANK HIMSELF TO DEATH AT THE WHITE Horse Tavern in 1953, the West Village landmark had been dispensing spirits for three-quarters of a century. And the previous tenant of the little three-story wood-frame building, the James Dean Oyster House, had already been serving beer to wash down their mollusks for a number of years before that. The land once belonged to the Earl of Abingdon— who is commemorated in the wedge-shaped park just up Hudson Street—back when the Village really was a village remote from the city at the island's southern tip. The bar's literary associations also long predate Thomas; the first structure on this corner site was a bookstore with a rooming house upstairs.

With an entire room a veritable shrine to its most celebrated former patron, the White Horse is still popularly considered something of a writers' hangout. Looking down on the patrons from above the bar is a mounted white horse-head sculpture and a dozen or so variously sized white horse figurines; the lights suspended from the ceiling are topped with white horse heads, and the glass door panels are etched with white horse-head silhouettes. The simple pub-fare menu — burgers, chili dogs, tuna melts, chicken pot pies — is posted on chalkboards. The seven draft beers include a White Horse ale, and there are ten bottled beers and two ciders. In good weather picnic tables are set out beneath umbrellas on the sidewalk.

IN BRIEF

HURLEY'S, 232 WEST 48TH STREET. A reincarnation of the 1892 pub that survived the construction of Rockefeller Center and lived in its shadow until it finally lost its lease, reopening with a vintage-style interior a few blocks away in 2000.

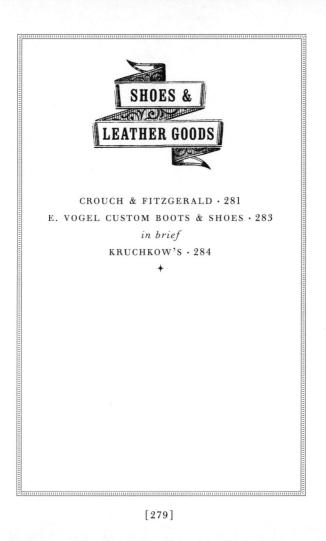

SHOES & LEATHER GOODS

✦

CROUCH & FITZGERALD

400 MADISON AVENUE (47TH STREET)
☎ (212) 755-5888
🚇 5TH AVE/53RD ST (E/V); 51ST ST (6)
MON-SAT: 9AM-6PM

✦

IN 1839, WHEN MESSRS. CROUCH AND FITZGERALD, TWO ENGLISHMEN NEW TO New York, opened their harness and luggage store at 1 Maiden Lane, some warned that the business, two blocks north of Wall Street, would surely fail because it was too far uptown. The shop prospered, however, at first outfitting traveling salesmen with sturdy leather sample cases to hold their wares. As mid-century improvements in ocean navigation and the railway system meant that more middle- and upper-class Americans looked to travel as an activity that would increase their social status, the company found its real success. All these new tourists needed luggage, and Crouch & Fitzgerald became the city's leading maker and retailer of steamer trunks.

After the Civil War, the firm was located in the exclusive shopping district centered around Union Square that would come to be known as the Ladies' Mile. Fitzgerald, the money man, had died in 1857; Crouch, the craftsman, carried on without him for almost 50 years. By then, the business, one of the first to be listed in the New York phone directory, operated a factory on West 41st Street and three shops, employing a total of 200 craftsmen and sales people. Among their eminent clients were the Roosevelt family, who had their luggage made especially for them at Crouch & Fitzgerald. Jackie Kennedy presented her husband with a monogrammed Crouch attaché case while he was still a senator; the company went on to make the leather case for the top hat he famously carried on the day of his inauguration.

The present store in Midtown — occupied since 1930 and now the only one remaining — no longer does custom work, but continues to sell Crouch-made briefcases as well as the luggage of Tumi, Hartman, Boyt, Halliburton, and other top manufacturers.

E. VOGEL
CUSTOM BOOTS & SHOES

19 HOWARD STREET
(BROADWAY-LAFAYETTE STREET)
☎ (212) 925-2460
🚇 CANAL ST (6/J/M/N/Q/R/W/Z)
MON-FRI: 8AM-4PM; SAT: 8AM-1PM

✦

ON RIOTOUS CANAL STREET, VENDORS HAWK KNOCKOFFS OF EVERYTHING FROM Rolexes to Chanel handbags. Ironically, half a block north, on the comparatively tranquil backwater of Howard Street, can be found E. Vogel, one of the last remaining purveyors in New York of handcrafted, one-of-a-kind, custom-made goods.

The shop, originally located at Centre and Grand Streets, was founded in 1879 by Egidius Vogel, a master cobbler from Wurtzburg, Germany; his great-grandsons run the business today. After nearly 100 years of operation, and a couple of local moves, the business settled in to its current location, a three-story brick building dating from 1872. The small showroom in front of the workshop, suffused by the spicy aroma of leather and polish, displays a selection of beautiful and very costly handmade shoes and riding boots. It would be easy to assume that the shop does a nice little trade in custom footwear for a select local clientele. In fact, Vogel sells several thousand pairs a year, relatively few out of this showroom. About 80 percent of its production is riding boots, and most are fitted and sold in tack shops across the country and around the world. The U.S. Equestrian Team wears Vogel, as do the national teams of Canada, England, France, and Japan. As have Charles Lindbergh, Jimmy Cagney, Jacqueline Kennedy Onassis, and the Sultan of Brunei.

While the company is most famous for its boots, Egidius happens to have introduced the low-cut wingtip to Wall Street businessmen in the early 1900s. Now classics, these and the other beautifully crafted shoes — for business, for walking, for golf — are available only here on Howard Street.

IN BRIEF

KRUCHKOW'S, FIFTH AVENUE (78TH-79TH STREETS), BAY RIDGE, BROOKLYN. Since 1907.

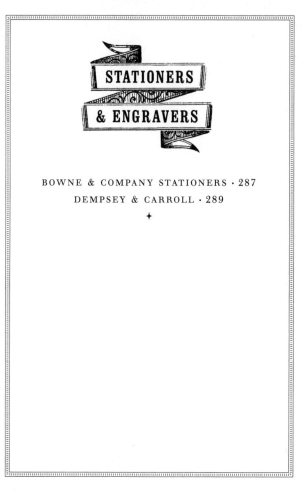

STATIONERS & ENGRAVERS

✦

BOWNE & COMPANY
STATIONERS

211 WATER STREET
(FULTON-BEEKMAN STREETS)
☎ (212) 748-8651
🚇 FULTON ST/BROADWAY NASSAU
(1/2/4/5/A/C/J/M/Z)
MON-SAT: 10AM-5PM

✦

THE MASSACHUSETTS COLONY, 1775: THE BATTLES OF LEXINGTON AND CONCORD began the American Revolution. In New York, war or no war, busy merchants in the bustling little port city needed supplies to conduct their business. That year, a Quaker named Robert Bowne opened a shop on Pearl Street that sold "Writing Paper, English and American; Account Books; Quills and Pens; Binding and Printing Materials; Bolting Cloth; Powder, Fur, Nails, Glass and Dry Goods; Pitch Pine Boards; and a few cases of low-priced Cutlery." Bowne & Company eventually narrowed its focus to become one of the finest printer-stationers in the city, offering in its first century such innovative products as chalk (1835), "paper cases," which came to be better known as envelopes (c. 1850), postal cards (c. 1872), and "paper tablets" or pads (c. 1876).

As the financial district took shape on nearby Wall Street, Bowne increasingly concentrated on the printing of stock certificates, prospectuses, and other essential documents, eventually becoming one of the leaders in the field.

In anticipation of its bicentennial, the firm funded, as part of the South Street Seaport Museum, a working nineteenth-century-style print shop. This enterprise, a stone's throw from Bowne's original location, is housed in a restored 1835 loft building that was originally occupied by a printer. Custom orders for wedding invitations, greeting cards, birth announcements, and more are printed at the back of the shop on several antique hand presses, including a restored Columbian adorned with an eagle on the counterweight (symbolic of the balance of power), a dolphin (representing speed and wisdom), and the figure of Hope, who rises whenever an impression is made. Blank books, bookplates, notepads, and limited-edition volumes of Edgar Allan Poe and Walt Whitman— printed with some of the 1,200 styles of nineteenth-century type in Bowne's collection— are among the many ready-made items also for sale.

DEMPSEY & CARROLL

110 EAST 57TH STREET
(PARK-LEXINGTON AVENUES)
☎ (212) 486-7526
🚇 59TH ST/LEXINGTON AVE (4/5/6/N/R/W)
MON-FRI: 10AM-6PM; SAT: 10AM-5PM

✦

FROM THEIR PRIVILEGED POSITION WITH-IN THE ELITE SOCIETY OF VICTORIAN NEW York, Edith Wharton and Henry James detailed the interactions of characters who lived according to complex rules of etiquette. Helping to promote as well as profit from the dread of violating this unforgiving protocol was Dempsey & Carroll, a firm of stationers and engravers located along with other prestigious shops such as Tiffany (p.189) on Union Square. Soon after Dempsey's 1878 opening, one of its catalogs offered grave warnings to bachelors on the proper procedure for leaving their calling cards when visiting young ladies with whom they were only recently acquainted. Crucial advice was also rendered on such delicate subjects as weddings, entertaining, and correspondence—for which the shop would provide the required hand-engraved announcements, invitations, seating charts, place cards, menu cards, personalized stationery, note cards, mourning paper, and much more.

For those who still value tradition, Dempsey & Carroll—now housed in a plush shop on East 57th Street—will advise on the correct arrangement of a monogram, that "Miss" is still the only suitable title on an unmarried woman's stationery, and that for wedding invitations white paper is simply not as tasteful as ecru. While fine ready-made items are available, the firm's specialty remains personalized stationery, engraved by hand from etched copper plates. These plates are retained in Dempsey & Carroll's workshop, lowering the cost of subsequent printings.

The shop also carries S.T. DuPont fountain pens, leather desk accessories, and diminutive Staffordshire boxes that can be custom-enameled with the likeness of a beloved house or pet.

See also: BERGDORF GOODMAN (P. 61), CARTIER (P. 187), TIFFANY (P. 189).

STEAK & CHOP HOUSES

✦

DELMONICO'S

55 BEAVER STREET (SOUTH WILLIAM STREET)
☎ (212) 509-1144   🚋 WALL ST (1/2)
MON-FRI: 7AM-10PM

✦

BEN WENBERG OWNED AND PILOTED SHIPS THAT PLIED THE WATERS BETWEEN NEW York and South America. He was also an amateur chef, and upon his return he would invariably drop in on his friends the Delmonicos, proprietors of the finest restaurant in America, and share with them his latest gastronomic discoveries. On one such occasion in 1876, he demanded a chafing dish, two large lobsters, a half-pound of butter, six eggs, a pint of heavy cream, and a glass of rum; he supplied his own hot chili peppers. The resulting dish produced an aroma so luscious it lured diners from their tables to investigate. By popular demand, lobster à la Wenberg soon appeared on the restaurant's vast menu.

Wenberg later slipped from the Delmonicos' good graces when he broke a strict house commandment against engaging in strident political argument. From then on, although he was allowed to enter the premises and was always politely seated, he never was served. As a final insult, the Delmonicos kept his popular creation on the menu but scrambled the letters of his name: from then on it was known as lobster à la Newberg.

The restaurant had been founded by Swiss immigrants Giovanni (John) and Pietro (Peter) Delmonico. In 1826 John was the captain of a trading schooner that was anchored in New York harbor while the city organized to celebrate the 50th anniversary of the American Revolution. Watching the preparations, he concluded that New York was a culinary wasteland. The following year he switched professions and bought a wine shop on the Battery. Its success enabled him to go back to Switzerland and fetch his older brother, Peter, a confectioner. Together, they opened a six-table establishment on William Street serving Continental sweets. Two years later they added hot meals — and a fetching female cashier — and their business took off. When their building was destroyed by the Great Fire of 1835, the brothers built a larger and far more luxurious restaurant on the corner of Beaver and William Streets. Over the years a number of locations farther uptown were opened and closed, but the Beaver Street Delmonico's remains, its grand entrance still flanked by twin columns of Pompeian marble.

In its heyday, Delmonico's menu listed nearly 350 items. The menu today is not nearly as extensive, but it still offers a wide selection for what is now considered a Wall Street steak house. There is, of course, Delmonico steak, sirloin, filet mignon, and porterhouse. There are three kinds of lamb chops, a veal chop, and several seafood choices, including that old standby, lobster Newberg. There's a nice range of vegetable dishes, and a dessert menu that includes flourless chocolate cake with Grand Marnier sabayon, cream cheese cake with fresh berry compote, a raspberry napoleon, and another dish invented by the house—to commemorate the 1867 purchase of arctic territory from Russia— Baked Alaska. For more casual dining, followed perhaps by cognac and a cigar, the cozy mahogany-paneled barroom beckons.

GAGE & TOLLNER

372 FULTON STREET (SMITH-JAY STREETS)
DOWNTOWN BROOKLYN
☎ (718) 875-5181
🚇 JAY ST/BOROUGH HALL (A/F)
MON-FRI: 11:30AM-3:30PM, 5PM-10PM
SAT: 3:30PM-11PM

✦

THE BROOKLYN BRIDGE, WHICH WAS SOON TO RENDER THE EAST RIVER FERRIES redundant, was under construction in 1879 when Charles M. Gage opened a dining establishment at 302 Fulton Street, not far from the towering eastern pier of the bridge. He was soon joined in the business by Eugene Tollner. Their aim was simple: to run the finest restaurant in town.

In 1892 they moved to a bigger and better location just down the street. The interior of the new place was as rich and elegant as the diners who frequented it — a guest list that over time included "Diamond" Jim Brady, Lillian Russell, Fanny Brice, and Mae West. The long dining room was inspired by Pullman dining cars of the Gilded Age, right down to the gentle curve where walls meet ceiling. The large arched mirrors were trimmed in cherry; the tables were of solid mahogany; the walls were covered with luxurious faux leather. There were graceful polished-brass gaslight chandeliers.

The building's Italianate exterior was landmarked in 1973, and two years later Gage & Tollner became the first restaurant in the city with a landmarked interior. Sadly, by 1995 the quality of food and service had plummeted, the building was in disrepair, and the owner — Messrs. Gage and Tollner were long gone — was heading for bankruptcy. A distinguished coalition of Brooklyn citizens and institutions brought in longtime local restaurateur Joe Chirico to keep the borough's oldest restaurant alive. With good advice and counsel, and substantial resources, Chirico restored the dining palace to its former glory. New carpeting was custom-loomed to match the old pattern; the tables and marble-topped oyster bar are restored originals, as are the gas chandeliers. In fact, every evening at seven o'clock there is a ritual in which the electric lights are dimmed and the gas lamps ceremoniously lit.

The food at Gage & Tollner — it calls itself an oyster and chop house — is classic American with a bit of a southern lilt. Offerings include oysters on the half shell, fried oysters atop a mushroom-fennel ragout, lobster salad with haricot verts, Charleston she-crab soup, crab cakes, soft clam bellies, shrimp or lobster Newberg, sweet potato fries, rack of lamb, filet mignon with shitake mushrooms, and an aged New York sirloin. Service is fast and friendly, and the waiters still famously wear insignias that show how long they've been in service. The wine list is extensive, with more than 75 reds, 40 whites, and 20 wines by the glass. The usual wine-producing locales are well represented, but there are also several selections that reveal an uncommon sense of East Coast history. There is, for instance, a cabernet sauvignon from Brotherhood in the Hudson Valley, the oldest winery in America, as well as Jefferson's Dream, a delightful Virginia chardonnay from the nation's oldest vitis vinifera plantation.

HARRY'S AT HANOVER SQUARE

1 HANOVER SQUARE (PEARL-STONE STREETS)
☎ (212) 425-3412   🚇 BOWLING GREEN (4/5)
MON-FRI: 11:30AM-10:30PM

✦

INDIA HOUSE. THE VERY NAME CONJURES IMAGES OF THREE-MASTED SCHOONERS arriving in the port of old New York laden with jewels and spices from the Orient. In fact, the lovely brownstone palazzo, built in 1851 for the Hanover Bank, did not gain its romantic name until 1914, when a society of shipping-industry leaders purchased the property as a private club.

Since 1875, the ground floor—actually half a flight down from the pavement—has been leased out as an eating and drinking establishment. Today, Wall Street movers and shakers gather at the long U-shaped bar as the subway rumbles just beneath their feet. With its electronic stock ticker and television tuned to the Bloomberg financial channel, Harry's at Hanover Square is a microcosm of downtown New York. Here in the oldest part of the city beats the very pulse of the world's non-stop technologically-driven financial markets.

The current occupant followed a couple of German restaurants. Harry Poulakakos—a beekeeper in his native Greece—took over the space in 1972 and created one of the most popular watering holes in the financial district. At lunch time and after work, regulars fill the large, comfortable barroom, with its vintage wooden paneling, leaded-glass windows, and a pristine replica of the original pressed-tin ceiling. Those wanting a more intimate experience reserve a table in the rear brick-walled dining rooms. Among the starters are platters from the raw bar—named the Amex, the NASDAQ, and the NYSE, in ascending order of size and price—chopped salad, smoked salmon, and shrimp scampi. Steaks include a porterhouse, rib-eye, sirloin, and Chateaubriand for two; veal chop, baby back ribs, rack of lamb, hamburger, grilled swordfish, striped bass, beer-battered cod and chips, and a variety of pastas complete the offerings.

The intact period rooms upstairs in India House proper are now also leased to a very fine restaurant named Bayard's, run by Harry's son, Peter.

KEEN'S STEAK HOUSE

72 WEST 36TH STREET (FIFTH-SIXTH AVENUES)
☎ (212) 947-3636
🚇 34TH ST/HERALD SQ (B/D/F/N/Q/R/W)
MON-FRI: 11:45AM-3PM, 5:30PM-10:30PM
SAT: 5PM-10:30PM; SUN: 4PM-8PM

✦

VISITING NEW YORK IN 1901, LILLIE LANGTRY, THE BRITISH STAGE SENSATION and mistress to King Edward VII, wanted to eat at Keen's, a theatrical haunt in the center of the Herald Square show-business district. Disregarding the "men only" notice, the Jersey Lily entered the restaurant, was seated, but was never served the mutton chop she ordered. Not one to shy away from publicity, the actress sued Keen's and won; women have been admitted to the restaurant ever since. The onetime thorn in the management's side is now honored with an upstairs room named for her.

J. P. Morgan, Stanford White, Florenz Ziegfeld, John Barrymore, Babe Ruth, and "Buffalo Bill" Cody are among the other notables who frequented Keen's and are remembered by their old pipes, which the restaurant displays in a glass case near the entrance. In fact, pipes—clay churchwarden pipes made in the Netherlands—are inseparable from the Keen's lore. More than 50,000 that regulars once checked with the house still hang from the ceilings despite the fact that for some time the law has prohibited smoking them.

Originally the restaurant was a part of the Lambs Club, the London-based theatrical association, until 1885, when Albert Keen, the manager, decided to run the English-style chophouse independently. Before the theater district moved up Broadway to Times Square, performers in costume and full stage makeup between acts continued to drop in at Keen's bar from neighboring playhouses, joining reporters and editors from the *New York Herald*'s offices around the corner. The crowded walls of the restaurant are a veritable museum of period theatrical memorabilia— sepia-toned photographs of turn-of-the-century performers in their greatest roles, woodcut billboards, and fading playbills. Among Keen's most valued treasures is what is purported to be Abraham Lincoln's actual program for *Our American Cousin* at Ford's Theater. This and an early newspaper account of the assassination, a reward bulletin, facsimiles of Lincoln's letters, and vintage political cartoons and caricatures hang in the second-floor room named in the president's honor. Teddy Roosevelt, a Keen's regular during his tenure as New York City police commissioner, is also remembered in the Bullmoose Room.

Keen's boasts one of the great old New York interiors. In the warm, dimly lit rooms, with their leaded-glass windows, burnished brass wall sconces, and blazing brick fireplaces, diners order from a traditional chophouse menu: New York sirloin, prime rib, aged porterhouse, filet mignon, and the gargantuan house mutton chop served with home-made mint jelly. Fresh oysters, Maine lobster, Maryland crab cakes, and fried chicken salad are also available. Among the old-style desserts are Keen's red berry bibble, coffee cantata, and Iowa caramel custard.

The bar, adorned with a portrait of a nude Ziegfeld girl, stocks nearly 200 single-malt scotches.

PETER LUGER

178 BROADWAY (DRIGGS AVENUE)
☎ (718) 387-7400   🚇 MACY AVE (J/M)
MON-THUR: NOON-9:45PM
FRI-SAT: NOON-10:45PM; SUN: 1PM-9:45PM
CASH ONLY

✦

MANY OF THE OLDEST SHOPS AND RESTAU-RANTS IN NEW YORK CITY ARE STILL OWNED by their founding familes. Others were inherited by a faithful employee. Peter Luger, the legendary steak house in Williamsburg, Brooklyn, ended up in the hands of a loyal customer.

When Peter Luger died in 1941, more than half a century after he had founded his German-style restaurant in 1887, his children wanted nothing more than to unload the old place, which had depended on the dwindling Brooklyn shipyards for most of its trade. They put the business up for public auction in 1950. Sol Forman, the owner of the metalworking plant directly across the street, was a regular who had entertained clients at Luger's daily for more than 25 years, sometimes eating there as many as ten times a week. On a lark, Forman sub-mitted a bid — the only bid — winning the historic eatery for the price of the real estate alone.

Although his wife, Marsha, had her doubts — the only thing they knew about restaurants, she pointed out, was eating in them — she threw herself into the new venture. With a retired government meat inspector in tow, Mrs. Forman spent countless early mornings in the wholesale meat market, learning to select only the finest sides of beef, which were then stored in the restaurant's own aging cellars. Her hard work paid off handsomely, for not only was Luger rescued from certain death, but it became what many people believe is the finest steak house in the country.

The Formans have now owned the restaurant for more than half a century. A second and third generation of women are in charge, with Jody Storch, Sol's granddaughter, making the crucial trips to the meat district. Aside from the addition of air conditioning, grilled salmon, and a salad, few changes have been made to the comfortable, unpretentious premises. The half-timbered walls, leaded-glass windows, sawdust-covered floors, Bavarian beer steins, and original well-worn oak tables still provide the perfect setting for the perfect New York meal: sliced-tomato-and-onion salad, shrimp cocktail, creamed spinach, french fries, and the best porterhouse steak imaginable. Many regulars feel a stop for a martini at the long vintage bar is an essential part of the visit. Those who do not consider steak de rigueur can opt for pot roast, prime rib, chicken or lamb chops, or corned beef and cabbage, all delivered by a staff of veterans, some of whom have been here since the 1960s. Desserts include apple strudel, cheesecake, fruit tarts, pecan pie, and the aptly named Holy Cow Hot Fudge Sundae — topped with a small chocolate heifer — all accompanied by a bowl of schlag, freshly whipped cream.

The famed Peter Luger steak sauce, which has been on the tables since before anyone can remember, is still a favorite; the restaurant's mail order department sells some 300 cases of the tomato-and-horseradish condiment each day. Tables at Luger are difficult to come by at both lunch and dinner, so reserve well in advance.

OLD HOMESTEAD

56 NINTH AVENUE (14TH-15TH STREETS)
☎ (212) 242-9040
🚇 14TH ST (A/C/E); 8TH AVE (L)
MON-FRI: NOON-11PM; SAT: 1PM-MIDNIGHT
SUN: 1PM-9:45PM

✦

AMONG THE MANY PARTS OF THE CITY CHARLES DICKENS TOURED DURING HIS 1868 visit to America was 14th Street, where he delivered a series of lectures at Steinway Hall, the auditorium of the piano manufacturer (p. 325) near Union Square Park and its fine shops. Although he would certainly have been taken with that elegant eastern end of the broad thoroughfare, the western portion of the street as it approached the Hudson River was another story. An unimpressed Mr. Dickens observed that there were "300 boarding houses in W. 14th St., exactly alike, with 300 young men, exactly alike, sleeping in 300 hall bedrooms, exactly alike, with 300 dress suits, exactly alike, lying on so many chairs, exactly alike, beside the bed." Farther west, Dickens would have met with the far more insalubrious wholesale meat market that had occupied the area for more than a century. Had he rounded the corner onto Ninth Avenue, though, the esteemed writer would have found a restaurant that opened that very year, catering to butchers from the market and serving a complete dinner for 12 cents.

The Old Homestead had been built on the site of the Tidewater Trading Post, an exchange for merchants arriving from points all along the Hudson who unloaded their wares at the boisterous waterfront piers. In 1868, an unknown Herman Melville was supporting himself as a customs inspector on those wharves but was likely too poor to afford the Homestead's bill of fare. For the first 50 years, the tiny restaurant was managed by the Heinz family — uncle and then nephew — who profited from their proximity to the market, procuring the choicest meat available. The place grew to eventually take over the adjoining properties and, along with the meat market, managed to survive many of the changes that long ago did away with businesses in less marginal areas.

In the last decade or so, this neighborhood, too, has become increasingly gentrified, with high-concept French brasseries and chic clothing shops opening along the aged cobblestone streets. The Old Homestead, too, has spiffed up, with a new décor that tips its hat to history with a new pressed-tin ceiling, hand-tinted photos of old New York, and vintage-style stained-glass lamps. Beef is still the order of the day, with choices including porterhouse, prime rib, filet mignon, sirloin, steak au poivre, and sliced steak with onions, mushrooms, and roasted peppers. French onion soup, oysters Rockefeller, beluga caviar, veal chops, rack of lamb, calves liver, free-range chicken, lobster, yellowfin tuna, and Chilean sea bass are among the other entrées.

ET CETERA

✦

BARCLAY-REX

75 BROAD STREET
(BEAVER-SOUTH WILLIAM STREETS)
☎ (212) 962-3355
🚇 BROAD ST (J/M/Z); WHITEHALL ST (N/R)
MON-FRI: 8AM-6:30PM; SAT: 9:30AM-5:30PM

✦

T HE REASON BROAD STREET IS SO BROAD IS THAT IT WAS ORIGINALLY A CANAL BUILT by the Dutch; ships would dock and disgorge their cargo into the heart of what was then New Amsterdam. The British later filled in the canal because of its pungent aroma at low tide.

Today it is worth a trip to Broad Street for the rich bouquet of cigar and pipe tobaccos at the city's oldest tobacconist — a fragrant island of calm in the heart of the financial district. The impression is that of a sleek, hushed mahogany library. A leisurely stroll reveals jar after jar of pipe tobacco, a collection of high-quality pipes, an assortment of smoking accessories, a wall of exotic imported cigarettes, and a well-stocked walk-in cigar humidor. In the lounge, visitors can smoke while they chat, sip a cappuccino, or read *The Wall Street Journal* in peace.

A closer inspection of the premises reveals a group of superb vintage briar pipes made in the

1940s by the hand of Vincent Nastri, the current proprietor's grandfather. A long-forgotten cache of them was discovered when Barclay-Rex packed up to move from Maiden Lane to its soigné new headquarters. Nastri, a pipe maker from Salerno, Italy, opened his first shop in 1910 on the corner of Barclay and Church Streets, just west of City Hall Park. "Barclay" designated the location; "Rex" paid tribute to his Great Dane, a neighborhood fixture in his red coat emblazoned with the name of the shop— an ingenious and inexpensive advertising device.

Nastri developed a signature line of pipes made of natural wood—no fillers to hide imperfections— with a light polish and wax; he did not believe in varnishes and stains. In 1949, the founder and his son, Vincent II, moved the shop to Maiden Lane, a few blocks from original site, and just down the street from Barthman Jewelers (p. 185). There it thrived for 51 years until Vincent III moved the business to its present location.

In addition to offering major commercial brands like Ashton, Castello, and Radici, the shop still produces its own line of pipes; as always, its craftsmen make repairs. Barclay-Rex carries fine pipe tobaccos of every description, including its own custom blends, some of which—such as Rexey (chocolatey and aromatic), No. 4 (blending Virginia and two types of Cavendish tobaccos), and No. 6 (like No. 4, but with the added punch of latakia and burley)—were formulated by the shop's founder. The business long ago expanded from pipes to cigars, which today represent 60 percent of the business. The big humidor stocks examples from every major maker, and features the Davidoff line.

Other locations: 70 E. 42nd Street, 570 Lexington Avenue, 3 World Financial Center.

BIDE-A-WEE

410 EAST 38TH STREET

(FIRST AVENUE-FDR DRIVE)

☎ (212) 532-4455

🚇 GRAND CENTRAL/42ND ST (4/5/6/7/S)

MON-SAT: 10AM-6PM; SUN: 10AM-5PM

✦

IN NINETEENTH-CENTURY NEW YORK, PRAC-
TICALLY EVERYTHING THAT MOVED WAS
moved by horse-drawn vehicles. Thousands of animals were bred every year and worked like any
other disposable commodity until they simply col-
lapsed in the streets from exhaustion. Such behavior
was routine before a number of groups for the
humane treatment of animals were formed.

Bide-A-Wee, named after a Scottish phrase that
means "stay awhile," was founded in 1903 by society
matron Mrs. Flora D'Aubry Jenkins Kibbe, who had
been inspired on a trip abroad by the benevolent
work of a French pet refuge that sent its Renault
ambulance throughout Paris to collect stray cats and
dogs. With the help of other prominent conscientious
New Yorkers, Mrs. Kibbe established this as one of
the first such rescue organizations in the city. Water
troughs and showers were provided for hot, thirsty
horses, and stray and unwanted pets were picked up,

brought to a shelter, and, if possible, placed in new, loving homes. No animal, unless it was terminally ill, was destroyed, a benevolence virtually unheard of in the United States at that time.

In the second decade of the twentieth century, after the shelter was evicted from its quarters near Gramercy Park — neighbors complained about the relentless barking — Bide-A-Wee relocated to its current site in a non-residential area near the East River. Additional facilities were opened on Long Island in Wantagh (1915) and Westhampton (1956), providing animal cemeteries for beloved pets along with veterinary care, obedience training, and rescue and adoption services.

Bide-A-Wee, which has placed more than one million companion animals in homes since its inception, relies entirely on public support for its funding. Adopting a puppy or kitten requires a $55 donation; adult dogs and cats $30. These fees include necessary vaccinations and spaying or neutering.

BROOKLYN WOMEN'S EXCHANGE

55 PIERREPONT STREET
(HICKS-HENRY STREETS), BROOKLYN HEIGHTS
☎ (718) 624-3435
🚇 BOROUGH HALL (1/2/4/5); COURT ST (N/R)
TUE-SAT: 10AM-4:30PM; THUR: 10AM-7PM

✦

WHEN THEIR EXHIBITORS WON A MEDAL FOR "FINE SEWING" AT THE PARIS EXPOsition of 1867, the Brooklyn Women's Exchange was already in its second decade of providing an outlet for the handiwork of needy women who were otherwise unable to earn a living outside their homes. The consignment shop, established by genteel ladies of means in Brooklyn Heights in 1854, also mobilized its members to make warm garments for the soldiers of the Civil War, the Spanish-American War, and the First World War. Henry Ward Beecher, the fiery abolitionist minister of the nearby Plymouth Church, bought clothing from the Women's Exchange to be distributed to the poor. And when President Lincoln was assassinated, the Exchange fashioned a commemorative flag that is now on extended loan to the Brooklyn Historical Society.

Today, the non-profit organization assists more than 350 disadvantaged or elderly craft workers—both men and women, from all over the country—by offering their wares for sale. In addition to hand-sewn linens and clothing, the merchandise includes hand-knit sweaters, hats, and blankets, dolls, stuffed animals and other toys, soaps, stationery, candies, and cookies. A special collection of garments, books, and artwork celebrating Brooklyn is very popular with the local clientele.

MOTT STREET GENERAL STORE

32 MOTT STREET
(BAYARD STREET-CHATHAM SQUARE)
☎ (212) 962-6280
🚇 CANAL ST (6/J/M/N/Q/R/W/Z)
DAILY: 8AM-6PM

✦

IN THE MID-NINETEENTH CENTURY, A SCANT
150 CHINESE MEN LIVED IN NEW YORK CITY
in the vicinity of Mott, Pell, and Doyer streets.
Around 1870, hundreds and eventually thousands
more arrived, many fleeing the racism and violence
directed against them on the American West Coast.
Although they were generally considered respectable
and law-abiding, there hung over this little colony a
malevolent aura of tong-war violence, opium dens,
and white slavery. As a consequence, immigration
laws were passed preventing these men from bringing over their wives and children.

This industrious society of bachelors started
businesses that required minimal capital and less
English. Hand laundries worked well, as did restaurants, especially "chop suey" houses serving a cuisine
that pretended to be authentic but was actually
invented in nascent Chinatown to attract adventurous

tourists. There were also souvenir shops, offering teapots, vases, figurines, and items made of exotic Chinese silk. In 1891, Lee Lok opened a shop called Quong Wuen Shing. The English name was the Mott Street General Store, now the community's oldest retail establishment. It stocked food, dry goods, bowls, chopsticks, whatever customers required. Its true function, however, was to serve as a post office, mail drop, bank, community center, and welcome wagon for Chinese immigrants. It was the place to go to hear the local news and gossip, to find out what was going on back home, to look for work, or to request help in times of need. The first location was on the west side of Mott Street. Eight years later the shop moved across the street to a six-story tenement building facing the 1801 Church of the Transfiguration.

The store still looks much as it did back then: the same portraits of Chinese ladies hang near the tin ceiling, the same pendulum clock ticks on the wall, and the same gloriously carved wooden arch still spans the old herb counter. Many of Chinatown's establishments once had carvings like this—valued both for their beauty and their ability to confound straight-flying evil spirits with twisting likenesses of peacocks and lucky fish—but the Mott Street General Store's is the only one remaining in public view today.

The shop may look the same, and it's still run by the founder's grandson, Paul Lee, but there has been one big change in recent years: computers, hidden behind the herb counter, make it possible for local customers (who, according to Mr. Lee, may not have bank accounts, and may not trust the mail) to pay their utility bills at the store. The service keeps them coming in, doing a little business, and exchanging news about the neighborhood and the folks back home.

THE NEW YORK EXCHANGE
FOR WOMAN'S WORK

149 EAST 60TH STREET

(LEXINGTON-THIRD AVENUES)

☎ (212) 753-2330

🚇 59TH ST/LEXINGTON AVE (4/5/6/N/R/W)

MON-SAT: 10AM-6PM

✦

IN THE EARLY SPRING OF 1878, MRS. WILLIAM G. CHOATE, INSPIRED BY THE example of the Brooklyn Women's Exchange (p. 318), invited some of her friends to meet in her parlor with the goal of establishing a charitable organization to assist needy women widowed in the Civil War. Like their socially conscious counterparts across the East River, the ladies of Manhattan would provide their less-fortunate sisters with "a market for the sale of any wares they would have it in their power to offer, which neither the stores nor any existing benevolent societies now furnish them." By 1883, this New York Exchange for Woman's Work, a non-profit consignment shop for highly skilled needlework and other finely crafted wares, had moved from the private home where it originally operated into the first of several store-front locations, adding in 1894 a catalog of the crafts, as well as a Collector's Corner for the sale of donated curios, jewelry, and the like.

One hundred-twenty years after its founding, the Exchange arrived at its current site across the street from Bloomingdale's. Here volunteers work to sell the handiwork of some 1,500 financially disadvantaged craftspeople—men's work was added in the 1970s. The specialties are toys, children's clothing, accessories, quilts, pillows, picture frames, and other decorative objects that have been crocheted, knitted, sewn, carved, whittled, painted, modeled, or decoupaged into the sort of one-of-a-kind wares seldom seen in the shops of Midtown Manhattan. Custom cakes, holiday pies, jams, and cheese straws are among the more popular food items.

STEINWAY & SONS

109 WEST 57TH STREET
(SIXTH-SEVENTH AVENUES)
☎ (212) 246-1100   🚇 57TH ST (F/N/R/Q/W)
MON-FRI: 9AM-6PM; SAT: 9AM-5PM
SUN: NOON-5PM

✦

FOR MOST NINETEENTH-CENTURY NEW YORKERS, AN EVENING'S ENTERTAINMENT was simply gathering around the piano in the front parlor and singing along to the popular tunes of the day. Piano showrooms were a common feature of the landscape, publishers of sheet music were the record labels of their day, and Steinway, the leading manufacturer of pianos, was a national icon.

In 1850 Henry Steinway—né Heinrich Steinweg—brought his large family from Germany to New York on the first steamship to cross the Atlantic. He was already well established as an instrument maker, but the unstable German economy made America seem a safer bet.

From the moment Steinway built his first American piano in 1853, demand exceeded supply. In 1860 he opened a mammoth new factory north of town in the frontier that is today Park Avenue and 53rd Street. By 1866 the company built the nation's premier concert hall, the 2,000-seat Steinway Hall on 14th Street near Union Square, just next door to their showroom. Many leading musicians of the day performed there, and in 1867 Charles Dickens, touring America, read to an adoring full house. In the early 1870s, the Steinway sons built a factory town in Astoria, Queens, complete with its own foundry, lumberyard, employee housing, church, library, trolley line, and ferry service.

The 14th Street buildings are long gone, but Steinways may be admired, touched, played, and purchased at Steinway Hall on 57th Street, less than a block from Carnegie Hall. Built at the peak of the company's success in the mid 1920s, and declared a landmark in 2002, this fascinating space is a mecca for piano enthusiasts. Behind the two-story rotunda, which usually showcases a majestic Model D nine-foot concert grand, is room after soundproof, temperature-and-humidity-controlled room of Steinways on display — grands, baby grands, and uprights in every finish imaginable.

IN BRIEF

KEENAN & BUCK, 36 WEST 44TH. When it opened in 1898, this optician outfitted turn-of-the-century New Yorkers with pince-nez, lorgnettes, and tortoise-shell spectacles. Today, the firm carries a good selection of quality frames and has a reputation for filling complex lens prescriptions

MAGER & GOUGELMAN, 345 EAST 37TH STREET. Peter Gougelmann, a Swiss ocularist—glass-eye maker—opened his New York practice in 1851. Three succeeding generations of Gougelmanns have aided tens of thousands of people, including such notables as Alfred I. DuPont, Jay Vanderbilt, Joseph Pulitzer, Helen Keller, Sammy Davis Jr., Hume Cronyn, Senator Thomas Gore, and Peter Falk.

CLAIRMONT NICHOLS, 1016 FIRST AVENUE. Not just eyeglasses but binoculars, telescopes, and all manner of optical gadgetry. Since 1885.

SPECIAL LISTINGS

Little Italy

✦

TriBeCa

✦

SoHo

✦

Greenwich Village

Queens

BROOKS 1890 RESTAURANT · 223

BOHEMIAN HALL · 241

CRESS FLORISTS · 125

EDDIE'S SWEET SHOP · 25

JAHN'S ICE CREAM PARLOR · 29

✦

Staten Island

BENNETT'S BICYCLES · 77

HOLTERMANN'S BAKERY · 32

F. LOMBARDI & SONS · 85

✦

*Note: Modell's Sports, Barnes & Noble, and
P.C. Richard & Son are chains with locations
throughout the boroughs.*

AUTHORS' FAVORITES

✦

INDEX

[337]

[339]

[340]

ACKNOWLEDGEMENTS

T HE AUTHORS ARE INDEBTED TO THE FOLLOW-
ING FOR THEIR GENEROUS PARTICIPATION:
Frank Adinolfi and Lenny Cristino (Monteleone's);
Bob Alleva (Alleva); Sabrina Balthazar (Hammacher
Schlemmer); Anthony Bamonte (Bamonte's); Georgia
Befanis and Shannon Cooney (Kiehl's); James
Benedetto and Anthony Scotto (Scotto's); George
Bennett and Doug Dicks (Bennett's Bicycles); Joan
Condron Borkowski (Billy's); Robin Boucher Benét,
Matthew Flood, and Jack Gallagher (Dempsey &
Carroll); Frank Buffa (Ferdinando's); Bill Butler, Jim
DiPaola, and Stephen Shlopak (Chumley's); Bill Carey
(Julius); Irving Chais (The Doll Hospital); Joe Chirico
(Gage & Tollner); Chris Christou and Valerie Christou
(George Taylor); Joe and Connie Citrano (Eddie's);
Elspeth Coleman and Herb Weitz (Weitz, Weitz &
Coleman); Matt Coltrin and Sasha Noe (Fanelli's);
James Conley (Keen's); Richard Cook (100 Year
Association); Tom and Laurie Cress (Cress Florists);
Rocco Damato (Bazzini); Sal Dell'Orto (Manganaro);
John DeRobertis (DeRobertis); Lou DiPalo and Marie
DiPalo (DiPalo); Joel Eichel and Ian Ginsberg
(Bigelow); Kim Hanley Esposito (P. J. Hanley); Robert
Esposito (Esposito's); Edward Faicco (Faicco's); Mark

Federman and Niki Federman (Russ & Daughters);
Curtis Gathje (The Plaza); Dean Georges (Irene Hayes
Wadley & Smythe Lemoult); Herbert Glaser (Glaser's);
Corrado Goglia (Delmonico's); Samuel M. Goldberg and
Alice Usdan (Mendel Goldberg); Henry P. Gougelmann
(Mager & Gougelman); Bill Gounaris (Brooks 1890);
Gary Greengrass (Barney Greengrass); Martin
Grubman (P. E. Guerin); Ronnie Hendler and Michael
Weisman (Hyman Hendler); Barbara Henry (Bowne &
Co.); Jeff Holtermann (Holtermann's); Marguerite
Howard (Bide-A-Wee); Michael Kapon (Acker, Merrall
& Condit); Karen Kinkaid (The Algonquin); Felice Kirby
(Teddy's); Danny Koch and Selma Koch (The Town
Shop); Renée Rosales Kopel (William Barthman); Seth
Kruchkow (Kruchkow's); Maresa Laino (Cartier); Dan
Lavezzo (P. J. Clarke's); Paul Lee (Mott Street General
Store); John Leonard (Leonard's); Danny Levine (J.
Levine); Bob Levy (Harris Levy); Scott Liroff (City
Knickerbocker); Mark Lobel (Lobel's); Mike Lombardi
(Lombardi & Sons); Peter Longo (Porto Rico); Jack
Lynch (Vogel); Anthony Macagnone (Lanza); Laura
Maioglio (Barbetta); Lloyd Malsin (Clairmont Nichols);
Marie McDonald (W. H. Jackson); Gerard Meagher
(Old Town); David Migden (Crouch & Fitzgerald); Joe
Miller (Miller's Harness); Dawn Minor (The New York
Exchange for Woman's Work); Eric Modell (Gerald
Modell); Mitchell Modell and Doris Tipograph

(Modell's Sports); Gregg Monsees and Warren Monsees (Putnam Rolling Ladder); Anthony Monte (Monte's); Vincent Nastri (Barclay-Rex); Paul Neuman (Rosedale); Kenneth Newman and Robert Newman (Old Print Shop); Frank, Jerry, Joe, and Peter Ottomanelli (O. Ottomanelli & Sons); Nick Ottomanelli (Ottomanelli Brothers); Jeff Pancer (Harry's for the Home); Leonard Pfluger Jr. (Keenan & Buck); Harry Poulakakos (Harry's at Hanover Square); Peter Poulakakos (Bayard's); Jim Puliatte (Bruno); Andrew Raffetto and Romana Raffetto (Raffetto's); Kenneth Reisdorf (Kenn's); Sally Robinson (Caswell-Massey); Kai Rosenthal (Schieffelin & Somerset); Anthony Russo (Gargiulo's); April Sack (The Tonic); Bob Sahadi (Sahadi); Tommy Sakas (Gramercy Park); Nathaniel Schoen (Garber); Larry Shar (Julius Lowy); Alyssa Shelasky (ABC Carpet); Gregg Sherry and Mark Sherry (Old Homestead); Nick Sitnycky (John's); Buster Smith (Pete's Tavern); Percy Sotomayor (A. T. Harris); Leo Spellman (Steinway & Sons); Steven Steinberg (New York Central); Jody Storch (Peter Luger); Kevin Sullivan (Beshar's); Thomas Sutherland (Neergaard Pharmacies); Carol Swedlow (Aronson's); Tony Tenneriello (Mare Chiaro); Carol Turner (Brooklyn Women's Exchange); Jerry Walker (Ear Inn, Walker's); Katherine Wankel (Wankel's); Cam Wiegmann (Henry Westpfal); Vincent "Buddy" Zeccardi (Roma); Robert Zerilli (Veniero's).

For their assistance, we also wish to thank Nadia Aguiar, Lana Bortolot, Nancy Campbell, Avery Corman, Joan Hartman, Ken Kobland, Eileen Morales and Bob Shamis of the Museum of the City of New York, Debrah Pearson, Ron and Barbara Schneider, Elizabeth Seder, and Gladys Yoblon.

✦

THE HISTORIC RESTAURANTS OF PARIS
A guide to century-old cafés, bistros, and gourmet food shops
Ellen Williams

The vanished world of 19th-century Paris awaits behind the doors of select restaurants and gourmet shops that have delighted customers for more than a hundred years. Crossing these thresholds, the discriminating diner and shopper can step into a gilded Belle Époque setting favored by Manet and Degas, a vintage confectioner that supplied bonbons to Monet, a shaded café terrace frequented by Zola. From tiny patisseries, cozy bistros, and rustic wine bars barely known outside each quarter to bustling brasseries, elegant tea salons, and world-famous cafés, this is an indispensable guide to classic cuisine served in settings of startling beauty. *"...in these elegantly designed pages you will discover...the café where Hemingway supped on garlicky port sausage, potatoes marinated in olive oil and a large stein of draft beer...tiled floors that lead to secret underground passageways or red velour banquettes beneath stained glass ceiling panels."*—Chicago Tribune. ISBN 1-892145-03-0 HARDCOVER $14.95

THE IMPRESSIONISTS' PARIS
Walking tours of the artists' studios, homes, and the sites they painted
Ellen Williams

Travelers who follow these walking tours will never see the paintings—or the city—in the same way again. From the historic neighborhoods along the Seine to the bustling grand boulevards to the cafés of Pigalle and the dance halls of Montmartre, this book pairs some of the world's beloved masterpieces with the exact locations where they were painted. The entertaining and informative text combines the history of art with anecdotes about the painters' lives and full-color reproductions as well as restaurant recommendations from the period. *"This pocketable hardcover book is a small marvel. It is fun to look at and fun to read."*—John Russell, The New York Times. ISBN 0-9641262-2-2 HARDCOVER $19.95

PICASSO'S PARIS
Walking tours of the artist's life in the city
Ellen Williams

Nearly a century after his arrival there as an unknown Spanish teenager, Paris still bears the mark of Pablo Picasso's enduring presence. This lively follow-up to the award-winning *The Impressionists' Paris* identifies the sites where Picasso created his masterpieces. Four walking tours follow the painter from the gaslit garrets of fin-de-siècle Montmartre to the Left Bank quarter where he sat out the Nazi Occupation. Along the way, meet his celebrated circle of friends, among them Gertrude Stein, Henri Matisse, and Coco Chanel. Dining recommendations include many of Picasso's favorite haunts: elegant brasseries off the Champs-Elysées, charming bistros in Saint-Germain, and the legendary cafés of Montparnasse. With full-color reproductions of Picasso's paintings, archival photos, vintage postcards, and maps. *"More detailed and informed than your typical travel book...the engaging writing and thorough research make for an excellent travel guide—or just a great read."* —Time Out New York.
ISBN 0-9641262-7-3 HARDCOVER $19.95

CITY SECRETS NEW YORK CITY
Robert Kahn, Editor & Series Editor
ISBN 1-892145-08-1 $24.95
Other titles in series: *City Secrets London, City Secrets Rome, City Secrets Florence, Venice and the Towns of Italy*
CLOTHBOUND $19.95

GARDEN GUIDE: NEW YORK CITY
Nancy Berner & Susan Lowry
Photographs by Joseph De Sciose
ISBN 1-892145-20-0 PAPERBACK $19.95

HERE IS NEW YORK
E.B. White
Introduction by Roger Angell
ISBN 1-892145-02-2 Hardcover $16.95

HARPO SPEAKS...ABOUT NEW YORK
Harpo Marx with Rowland Barber
Introduction by E. L. Doctorow
ISBN 1-892145-06-5 Hardcover $16.95

A HOUSE ON THE HEIGHTS
Truman Capote
Introduction by George Plimpton
ISBN 1-892145-24-3 Hardcover $16.95

THE LITTLE BOOKROOM
1755 BROADWAY, FIFTH FLOOR, NEW YORK NY 10019
PHONE 212 293 1643 FAX 212 333 5374
EDITORIAL@LITTLEBOOKROOM.COM
WWW.LITTLEBOOKROOM.COM

ELLEN WILLIAMS is the author of *The Historic Restaurants of Paris*, *Picasso's Paris*, and the award-winning *The Impressionists' Paris*. She edited Alexander Liberman's *The Artist In his Studio* and *Keith Haring Journals*. She was born in Greenwich Village, where she lives with her daughter.

STEVE RADLAUER is the author or co-author of five books and numerous articles for a range of publications including *New York* magazine, *Esquire*, *Spy*, *The New York Times*, and *The Los Angeles Times*. He is a native New Yorker.

Library of Congress Cataloging-in-Publication Data
Williams, Ellen. The historic shops & restaurants of New York:
a guide to century-old establishments in the city / Ellen
Williams and Steve Radlauer. p. cm. ISBN 1-892145-15-4
1. Restaurants—New York—New York (City)—Guidebooks. 2. Stores,
Retail—New York—New York (City)—Guidebooks. I. Title: Historic shops
and restaurants of New York. II. Radlauer, Steve, 1948- III. Title.
TX907.3.N72 N487 2002 647.95747'1—dc21 2002008554

The spelling of food items reflects that of individual establishments.

ISBN-13: 978-1-892145-15-4
ISBN-10: 1-892145-15-4

Printed in the United States of America
10 9 8 7 6 5 4 3 2

The Little Bookroom
1755 Broadway, Fifth Floor, New York NY 10019
T (212) 293-1643 F (212) 333-5374
editorial@littlebookroom.com
www.littlebookroom.com